obsessive-compulsive disorder

third edition

the facts

PADMAL DE SILVA

Institute of Psychiatry, King's College,
University of London
South London and Maudsley National
Health Service Trust, London

STANLEY RACHMAN

Psychology Department,
University of British Columbia,
Vancouver

OXFORD
UNIVERSITY PRESS

OXFORD
UNIVERSITY PRESS

Great Clarendon Street, Oxford OX2 6DP

Oxford University Press is a department of the University of Oxford.
It furthers the University's objective of excellence in research, scholarship,
and education by publishing worldwide in

Oxford New York

Auckland Cape Town Dar es Salaam Hong Kong Karachi
Kuala Lumpur Madrid Melbourne Mexico City Nairobi
New Delhi Shanghai Taipei Toronto

With offices in

Argentina Austria Brazil Chile Czech Republic France Greece
Guatemala Hungary Italy Japan South Korea Poland Portugal
Singapore Switzerland Thailand Turkey Ukraine Vietnam

Published in the United States
by Oxford University Press Inc., New York

© Oxford University Press 2004

The moral rights of the authors have been asserted

Database right Oxford University Press (maker)

First edition published 1992
Second edition published 1998
Third edition first published 2004
Reprinted 2005 (twice), 2006

A catalogue record for this title is available from the British Library

Library of Congress Cataloging in Publication Data
(Data available)

ISBN–13: 978–0–19–852082–5
ISBN–10: 0–19–852082–4 (Pbk)

4

Typeset by Cepha Imaging Pvt. Ltd., Bangalore, India
Printed in Great Britain
on acid-free paper by
Clays Ltd, St Ives plc

preface

This book is intended to provide the reader with basic information about obsessive–compulsive disorder. This is a relatively common anxiety disorder seen in clinics and hospitals, and is more widespread than had been traditionally assumed. Some recent surveys have shown a lifetime prevalence rate of up to 2 per cent in the general population. However, it is only the more severely afflicted who come for help.

We have been involved in the study and treatment of obsessive–compulsive patients for many years. In our clinical practice, we found the lack of a basic book that could be recommended to sufferers and their families to be a major handicap. This led us to the writing of this book, and its first edition was published in 1992. We hoped that sufferers of the disorder, and their families and friends, would find it of some use. We also hoped that the general reader interested in finding out about this fascinating disorder would find it useful. The response to the book from readers, both sufferers and others, has been most encouraging. An updated second edition was published in 1998. For the present—third—edition, we have revised the book extensively, bringing in new material so that it reflects up-to-date knowledge.

Research in the past thirty years has thrown much light on obsessive–compulsive disorder, and we have attempted to give a summary of some of the findings. A great deal more is known about this disorder today than was understood in the 1950s and the 1960s. However, many unanswered questions still remain. We have deliberately refrained from attempting to give simple answers to these questions; to have done so would have been misleading.

Much of what is said about the treatment of obsessive–compulsive disorder in these pages reflects a psychological orientation. This is particularly because of our own professional training but, more importantly, because the psychological approach has provided the most effective therapeutic strategies to help those who have these problems. Current and future research will no doubt lead to the refinement of the existing therapeutic strategies and the development of new ones. It will also throw more light on aetiology and other questions. Like everyone else in this area, we eagerly await these developments.

Note

Because of the problem of gender in the English Language, we have had to decide whether to use 'he', 'she', or 'person' when referring to people. Different authors have different practices, and we are aware that some people have strong views on this issue. For ease of reading, we have retained the more conventional, male form.

London and	P. de S.
Vancouver	S. R.
March 2004	

acknowledgements

We wish to thank Dona de Silva for her excellent secretarial help, and Roz Shafran and Adan Radonsky for their assistance in finding some key information. We also wish to express our gratitude to the staff of Oxford University Press for their valuable advice, and to our many colleagues, past and present, who have contributed to our thinking on the subject covered in this book.

contents

1
Obsessive–compulsive disorder: what is it?

Obsessive–compulsive disorder has been traditionally regarded as a 'neurotic disorder', like phobias and anxiety states. Other terms used for this disorder include: 'obsessive (or obsessional)–compulsive neurosis' and 'obsessive (or obsessional)–compulsive illness'—or simply 'obsessive (or obsessional) disorder' or 'compulsive disorder'. People with this problem can suffer considerable distress, and often feel that they are helpless victims. Although neurotic disorders are generally considered to be less handicapping and disabling than 'psychotic' illness—such as schizophrenia—severe obsessive–compulsive disorder sometimes causes major incapacitation and drastically affects people's lives.

Broadly speaking, neurotic disorders, or neuroses, are relatively minor psychiatric illnesses. The neurotic patient is aware that he has a problem—that is, he has insight. His contact with the outside world is relatively intact. In contrast, psychotic disorders, or psychoses, are more serious mental illnesses. The psychotic patient may have no insight that something is wrong with him, and his contact with the outside world may be severely impaired.

The terms 'neurotic disorders' and 'neuroses' are not widely used any more. In current psychiatric thinking, obsessive–compulsive disorder is classified as an 'anxiety disorder'. Other anxiety disorders include, among others, phobias, panic disorder, and generalized anxiety disorder; they all share anxiety as a basic feature, and there is overlap of symptoms among them. The categories of anxiety disorders are given in Table 1.

What is meant when someone is described as having an obsessive–compulsive disorder? The person displays and/or complains of either obsessions or compulsions or both, to a degree that affects his everyday functioning or causes him distress. Diagnosis of the condition is usually made on this basis. This is reflected in the generally agreed diagnostic criteria (Table 2).

Table 1 Anxiety disorders

Panic disorder, with or without agoraphobia
Agoraphobia, without a history of panics
Social phobia
Specific phobia
Generalized anxiety disorder
Obsessive–compulsive disorder
Post-traumatic stress disorder
Acute stress disorder

What are obsessions?

An obsession is an unwanted, intrusive, recurrent, and persistent thought, image, or impulse. Obsessions are not voluntarily produced, but are experienced as events that invade a person's consciousness. They can be worrying, repugnant, blasphemous, obscene, nonsensical, or all of these.

Table 2 Summary of criteria widely used for the diagnosis of obsessive–compulsive disorder

1. The person must have either obsessions or compulsions or both.
   (a) *Obsessions* are recurrent, persistent ideas, thoughts, images, or impulses that intrude into consciousness and are experienced as senseless or repugnant. They form against one's will, and the person usually attempts to resist them, or get rid of them. The person recognizes that they are his own thoughts. They also cause marked anxiety or distress
   (b) *Compulsions* are repetitive, purposeful forms of behaviour that are carried out because of a strong feeling of compulsion to do so. The goal is to prevent or reduce anxiety or distress, or to prevent some dreaded event or situation. However, the activity is not connected in a realistic way with what it aims to prevent, or it is clearly excessive. The person generally recognizes the senseless-ness of the behaviour and does not get pleasure from carrying out the activity, although it provides a relief from tension. Compulsions are usually performed according to certain rules, or in a stereotyped fashion
2. They are not due to another disorder, such as schizophrenia, depression, or organic mental disorder
3. The obsessions and/or compulsions cause distress to the person and/or interfere with his life and activities

The person neither wants nor welcomes them: instead, he usually resists them and tries to get rid of them. An obsession is a passive experience: it happens to the person. He may be engaged in some activity, like reading a book or driving a car, when the obsession intrudes into his consciousness. It disrupts his normal thinking and behaviour.

Some examples obsessions are as follows:

1. A young woman had the recurrent intrusive thought that her husband would die in a car crash. She also had vivid visual imagery accompanying this thought: she would 'see' the scene of the accident, the two cars, the broken glass, the blood, and the people involved.

2. A young woman had the recurrent intrusive thought that she was contaminated by dirt and germs from strangers.

3. A man had the recurrent intrusive doubt that he may have knocked down someone crossing the road.

4. Young married woman had the recurrent intrusive impulse to strangle children and domestic animals. This would be followed by the thought or doubt that she might actually have done this.

5. A young man had the recurrent intrusive thought 'Christ was a bastard'. He also felt an impulse to shout this out during prayer or a church service.

6. A young woman had the recurrent intrusive thought that she might offend people by touching them in a sexual, inappropriate manner.

7. A young man had recurrent intrusive images of himself violently attacking his elderly parents with an axe. He also had the thought that he might actually commit this act. This experience included images of the victims, of blood flowing, and of injuries caused.

8. A young woman had the recurrent, intrusive impulse to harm herself by burning her eyes with a lighted cigarette. This was accompanied by vivid visual images of the act.

9. A 14-year-old girl had the recurrent impulse to blurt out obscenities in public. She also had the thought that she might actually do, or have done, this.

10. A young woman had the recurrent thought that she would not survive beyond the age of 28.

These examples illustrate the main features of an obsession. It intrudes into consciousness, as an unwelcome outsider. It may take the form of a thought, an image, an impulse, or a combination of these. Obsessions in the form of thoughts are much more common than those in the form of impulses or images. When the obsession occurs, the person usually resists it, and tries to dismiss it. If he succeeds in dismissing it, it may well come back within a short period of time. Some patients report that their obsessions are with them most of their waking hours, despite desperate struggles to get rid of them. The effort involved in attempting to subdue obsessions can be exhausting, even though the struggle is not evident to friends and relatives. For some it feels as if the obsession is always there, hovering at the back of their minds.

The patient does not regard the obsessional thought, image, or impulse as something originating from outside: he recognizes and acknowledges that it is his own thought. This is an important feature since, in certain mental illnesses, patients may have the experience of thoughts having been put into their heads by outside agents. Obsessions are not experienced in this way.

Different uses of the word 'obsession'

It should be noted that meaning of the term 'obsession' in the context of obsessive–compulsive disorder is different from its meaning in day-to-day language. We often hear someone being described as 'obsessed with his job', and expressions such as 'He is obsessed with her', 'Football is an obsession with him', and so on. What is meant in such instances is that the person in question has an unusually great interest in something or someone, so that everything else pales into insignificance. But such an attachment, interest, or preoccupation is not seen by him as unwanted or unacceptable, and there is no resistance nor any attempt to dismiss it. Nor is it something that keeps intruding periodically into the person's mind. This is very different from the way the term 'obsession' is used in reference to obsessive–compulsive disorder. Both senses are related to the meaning of the Latin verb *obsidere* ('to besiege') from which the word 'obsession' is derived.

Some key features of obsessions

What are the contents of obsessions? There are three common themes: unwanted thoughts of aggression/harm, unwanted sexual thoughts, and blasphemous thoughts. Occasionally they are senseless and trivial, such as advertising jingles. An example of one of the latter came from a man who complained of the recurrent intrusive thought: 'These boys when they were young.' A woman had intrusive visual images of asymmetrical objects and patterns she had seen, which would come to her repeatedly. In some cases, the obsession consists of a doubting thought, which can apply to most things that the person does. For example, a young woman complained that, whenever she performed any action, she would immediately be assailed by the thought 'Did I do it right?' or 'Have I done the right thing?'

These are examples of obsessions with an aggression/harm theme. The person repeatedly has the unwanted, unwelcome thought of harming elderly people, say by pushing them in front of oncoming traffic or of attacking or molesting children. Obsessions often raise a fear of losing control, e.g. 'What if one day I lose control and harm a child? I must take great care to avoid being alone with a child'. Sexual obsessions often include recurrent images as well as thoughts of repugnant unacceptable sexual wishes or acts, such as incestuous thoughts, molesting children, and images of sexual exhibitionism. As with the aggressive obsessions, those with sexual content often arouse a fear of losing control, which, in turn, leads to avoidance of the people or places that are associated with the obsessions. Blasphemous obsessions, such as having obscene thoughts about sacred figures or shrines, can be extremely repugnant and give rise to tormenting episodes of self-doubt and self-criticism. 'I must be a total hypocrite to have these recurrent thoughts while seeming to be a righteous and religious person.'

It is probable that obsessions develop when the affected person mistakenly attaches great personal significance to the uninvited and repugnant thoughts that virtually everyone experiences from time to time; whereas most people dismiss these thoughts as nonsensical and insignificant, some highly sensitive people regard them as being important. If the affected person interprets the intrusive thoughts as being personally revealing and highly significant, then they tend to recur over and over again.

There is a strong tendency to conceal these recurrent and repugnant thoughts, mainly because the affected person anticipates, usually incorrectly, that if other people learn about these thoughts they, too, would interpret them as being revealing and highly significant. 'If other people really knew about my ugly thoughts they would recoil and brand me a monster.' One patient described his aggressive and sexual obsessions as 'my ugly little secret'. The mistaken interpretations made by patients who are tormented by obsessions generally lead to one or all of these conclusions about their 'deep, true character'—it means that 'I am mad, bad, or dangerous or all three of these'.

Obsessions produce internal resistance which can take various forms, such as endlessly debating with oneself, praying repeatedly, trying to neutralize or wipe out the thoughts, or even escaping completely from the situation in which the thought is experienced. Obsessions can also lead the patient to avoid other people.

Thought–action fusion

In some, an intrusive thought becomes significant because of a tendency to regard thoughts as being psychologically equivalent to the corresponding action. Thus, having the thought 'I may strangle someone' is seen as being as bad as actively strangling a person; there is a moral equivalence. A related tendency is to believe that, because one has had a thought about a misfortune or disaster, the likelihood of that misfortune actually occurring is increased. These factors, termed 'thought–action fusion', can lead someone to be very distressed about his intrusive thoughts, and thus to attach great significance to them. These thoughts then become recurrent clinical obsessions that affect the person.

What are compulsions?

A compulsion is a repetitive and seemingly purposeful behaviour that is performed according to certain rules or in a stereotyped fashion. It may be wholly unacceptable or, more often, partly acceptable. The behaviour is not an end in itself, but is usually intended to prevent some event or situation. However, the activity is not connected in a logical or realistic way with what it is intended to achieve (for example, touching a relative's photograph a certain number of times, in order to ensure that no harm comes to the relative), or it may be clearly excessive (such as washing hands for half an hour at a time to get rid of germs, or checking the door handle over a dozen times to make sure the door is firmly locked). There are also instances where the person engages in the compulsive act simply to ward off great anxiety, or even panic. The act is preceded or accompanied by a sense of subjective compulsion—that is, the person feels a strong urge to engage in the behaviour. Usually, there is a desire to resist. The person recognizes the senselessness or irrationality of the behaviour, although this may not always be so. No pleasure is derived from carrying it out, although it provides a release of tension or a feeling of relief in the short term.

Some examples of compulsions are as follows:

1. A young woman repeatedly and extensively washed her hands to get rid of contamination by germs. The washing was done in an elaborate ritual, six times without soap and six times with soap, on each occasion.

2. A young man checked door handles, gas taps, electric switches every time he went past them.

3. A 15-year-old girl cleaned and washed the area around her bed, including the wall, every night before going to bed, in order to rid it of germs and dirt.

4. A man opened letters he had written and sealed, to make sure that he had written the correct things. He would rip open the envelope, reread the letter, and put it into a new one several times before posting it.

5. A woman in her forties complained that every time she entered a room she had to touch the four corners of it, starting from the left.

6. A young man had the compulsion to touch with the left hand anything he had touched with the right hand, and vice versa.

7. A young man had the compulsion to empty his bladder before each meal. Even if he had urinated a short while before, he would go and empty his bladder prior to sitting down to the meal. He felt that otherwise he would not be able to enjoy his meal.

8. A young man had the compulsion to look back over his shoulder at any building that he was leaving. He would first look back over his left shoulder, then over his right, and then again over his left.

9. A young woman had the compulsion to wipe, with a wet cloth, all tables and worktops several times, each time that she was to use them. She did this to get rid of what she called 'invisible food particles'.

10. A 35-year-old married woman had the compulsion to wash and disinfect herself and her clothes, out of fear of contracting cancer. She spent many hours each day doing this.

The key feature of all these examples is that the person feels a strong urge—compulsive urge—to engage in a particular behaviour, which he carries out despite resistance and despite recognizing that it is irrational or excessive.

The avowed purpose in most instances is to prevent a misfortune or avoid harm, and the person feels a special responsibility for these preventive acts.

Contamination: dirt and disease

Feelings of contamination fall into two main categories: those in which the person feels contaminated by contact with dirty and disgusting material, and contamination arising from actual or threatened contact with material or people capable of transmitting infectious diseases to the person. It is a persistent, intense feeling of having been polluted or infected by physical contact with, or by association with, a place or person that is soiled, impure, infectious—or a combination of these. Contamination is accompanied by unpleasant emotions, among which disgust, fear, immorality, and shame are prominent. The person usually feels that the contamination can be transmitted to other people and, in these instances, will go to great lengths to avoid spreading the contamination. These contaminations instigate attempts to remove the dirt, impurity, or potentially infectious material. As a secondary consequence, it leads to extensive avoidance of situations in which the person fears that there is the possibility of contact with a contaminant. Intensive, meticulous, repetitive washing and cleaning compulsions are undertaken in an attempt to remove the feeling of dirtiness and/or the perceived threat to one's health. Compulsive cleaning is one of the most common, classical, manifestations of obsessive–compulsive disorder.

Covert compulsions

All the examples cited above are of overt compulsive behaviour—that is, behaviour involving bodily actions; but some compulsions are covert, or mental. Unfortunately, many writers on obsessive–compulsive disorder, and many doctors, psychologists, and psychiatrists, still tend to assume that compulsions are necessarily overt behaviour. They consider obsessions to be mental events, and compulsions to be overt, motor events. This division is incorrect. It is certainly true that obsessions are mental events, but not all compulsions are motor behaviour. Many patients have covert, or mental, compulsions that have all the main features of overt compulsions.

Here are some examples:

1. A man had the compulsion to say silently a string of words whenever he heard or read of any disaster or accident.

2. A middle-aged woman, who was distressed by the intensive repetitive appearance in her consciousness of obscene words, carried out a compulsive ritual each time this happened. This consisted of changing these words into similar but acceptable ones—for example, 'well' for 'hell'—and saying them silently four times.

3. A middle-aged man had the compulsion to visualize everything that was said in conversation to him, and what he was going to say in reply. He would not reply until he had obtained these visual images. Often this would take time, leading to long silences that were puzzling to others.

4. A woman, who was tormented by intrusive repetitions of bloody images of her relations and friends, felt compelled to reform those images, with the people concerned appearing to be in good health.

5. A young woman became very worried if she set her eyes on black objects, especially before going to sleep. When this happened she had the obsessional thought that it would cause her to go blind, or lead to some other disaster. So every time she experienced this, she felt compelled to visualize an object of a different colour, usually white, as a way of preventing these ill effects.

6. A young woman, who had the recurrent obsessional thought that she was responsible for any murders that she read or heard about, engaged in the compulsion of silently saying 'I did not do it' seven times, each time such a thought came.

These examples should make it clear that compulsions are not exclusively motor behaviour, but can be mental acts as well. Covert compulsions are also referred to as 'cognitive rituals' or 'cognitive compulsions'.

The active nature of compulsions

A feature of compulsions that needs to be stressed here is that a compulsion is actively brought about by the patient: he is not happy about doing it, but it is essentially his voluntary action, performed as a result of his compulsive urge, and not an automatic behaviour. Thus it is different from tics and muscle spasms that are found in some people, especially children, which are essentially involuntary motor responses. These are not actively, deliberately produced by the patient, thus making them different from compulsions. Unlike compulsions, they are not purposeful.

Resistance

Obsessions and compulsions are generally resisted. At one time it was considered by many experts that resistance was an essential feature of obsessive–compulsive disorder. However, we now know that this not always the case. Although in the vast majority of cases the person does resist the obsession or the compulsive urge, there are exceptions, particularly with regard to compulsions. It appears that in the early stages of the disorder a person resists his compulsive urges strenuously, but after repeated failures over a period of time, he may begin to show much less resistance. Patients with strongly established, chronic obsessive–compulsive problems may experience little or no resistance to the obsessions or the compulsive urges. They have yielded to them.

Different uses of the word 'compulsion'

As with the term 'obsession', our use of the term 'compulsion' here is different from, and more specific than, the way it is used in everyday language. We often hear people talking about 'compulsive lying', 'compulsive eating', 'compulsive gambling', and so on. These types of behaviour are different from the kinds of compulsions that we are concerned with here. As noted above, compulsions are acts that are the result of an urge that the person usually tries to resist, and which are carried out reluctantly. They are seen as essentially irrational or senseless, and give no pleasure or satisfaction. Forms of behaviour such as compulsive gambling do not show these features—although they are problems in their own right, they are not part of obsessive–compulsive disorder.

Sometimes the term 'compulsive' is used for behaviour such as repeatedly touching one's forehead, or recurrent nail-biting, thumb-sucking, and hair-pulling. These are habits, and the person usually engages in them, at least part of the time, without being aware of them. They lack the characteristic features of the compulsion in obsessive–compulsive disorder, such as purposefulness and meaningfulness. True compulsions are carried out in order to accomplish some aim; behaviours such as nail-biting, hair-pulling, and so on, are not, nor do they provoke a feeling of resistance. These kinds of behaviour are best seen as habits rather than true compulsions, since their similarity to the latter is superficial.

Putting matters right

An unusual, flexible type of compulsive behaviour consists of a powerful urge to 'put matters right'—typically, to place one's belongings in a particular place or order in a rigidly prescribed manner, or to ensure that one's appearance is exactly right, and so on. There are also covert forms of this compulsion.

> A 28-year-old man spent up to five hours per day combing and brushing his hair 'to get it right', and felt extremely uncomfortable until he succeeded. Whenever he left his home he wore a cap to conceal his hair, except on rare occasions when it felt right.

The urge to put matters right is closely associated with the compulsion to arrange and order one's possessions (books, clothes, papers). This can take many hours and must be satisfactorily completed before leaving or before starting on a fresh task. Intense ordering and arranging is more noticeable in child obsessive–compulsive disorder than in adult cases, perhaps because other and more severe compulsions arise in adulthood to overshadow the compulsion to order and arrange. People, young or old, who feel compelled to introduce and maintain inflexible order can react strongly if their 'systems' are disrupted. The drive for order can be associated with the comparable compulsion to introduce symmetry and exact balances, mainly pertaining to one's possessions.

A self-report scale for assessing the compulsions to order and arrange has been developed recently, and is reproduced in Appendix 5.

The diagnosis of obsessive–compulsive disorder

As mentioned earlier, a person may be considered to have an obsessive–compulsive disorder if he experiences or displays obsessions or compulsions, or both (see p. 2). However, it is necessary to add an important qualification: it is not the presence of obsessions and/or compulsions as such that matters, but the degree to which they cause distress and/or interfere with the person's life. This is an additional requirement in the diagnostic criteria cited in Table 2 (see p. 2). In the following paragraphs, we shall try to make clear why this qualification is necessary.

Obsessions and compulsions in the general population

It is important to realize that obsessions and compulsions are not uncommon in the general population. There are many people who have obsessions and/or compulsions, but never go to a clinic or hospital seeking help.

Normal obsessions

Several research studies carried out in different centres have shown that many people, randomly selected from the general population, in fact about four-fifths of them, admit to having obsessions. These obsessions are no different in either form or content from the obsessions of patients who seek help. The differences are quantitative: the non-patients tend to have obsessions less frequently, their distress as a result of them is less severe, and so on. In a study carried out in London some years ago, we asked a random sample of people to report their obsessions, if they had any. Here are some of the obsessions they described:

- thought of an accident occurring to a loved one;
- thought of harm befalling her children, especially accidents;
- thought that the chances of an air crash involving herself would be minimized if one of her relatives had such an accident;
- thought that she might commit suicide;
- image of her parents lying dead;
- thoughts of 'unnatural' sexual acts;
- impulse to jump off the platform in front of an approaching train;
- impulse to attack violently and kill a dog;
- impulse to do something (e.g., shout or throw things) to disrupt the peace at a gathering;
- impulse to harm innocent people (e.g., children, elderly people);
- impulse to shout obscenities.

As can be seen, these are similar to the obsessions commonly reported by obsessive–compulsive patients.

Normal compulsions

Similarly, a large proportion of normal people have compulsions. Various forms of checking behaviour are quite commonplace. Consider, for example, a man who goes round the house checking to make sure that all gas taps are closed, before leaving home; or a woman who goes once or twice to the kitchen she has just left in order to check that the oven is switched off. No one would seriously describe them as having an obsessive–compulsive disorder requiring help. Many people have minor compulsive rituals, such as always putting on the left shoe first, or arranging the desk in a certain way. Studies have shown that such compulsions are not uncommon in the general population.

An excellent account of a compulsion in a normal person is provided in Boswell's biography of Samuel Johnson, the great eighteenth-century man of letters. Boswell commented on various 'singularities' or 'particularities' of Johnson:

> He had another particularity, of which none of his friends ever ventured to ask an explanation. It appeared to be some superstitious habit, which he had contracted early, and from which he had never called upon his reason to disentangle him. This was his anxious care to go out or in at a door or passage by a certain number of steps from a certain point, or at least so as that either his right or his left foot (I am not certain which) should constantly make the first actual movement when he came close to the door or passage. Thus I conjecture: for I have upon innumerable occasions, observed him suddenly stop, and then seem to count his steps with a deep earnestness; and when he had neglected or gone wrong in this sort of magical movement, I have seen him go back again, put himself in a proper position to begin the ceremony, and, having gone through it, break from his abstraction, walk briskly on, and join his companion.

Superstitions

There are similarities between superstitious ideas and some obsessions, and between superstitious acts and compulsive behaviour. Superstitions and certain obsessions are similar in that the person recognizes the irrationality of the idea, or its associated activity, but prefers to err on the side of caution or safety. Like compulsions, many superstitious acts are carried out in order to prevent a misfortune from happening. However, there are also many superstitious acts that are carried out in order to enhance the probability of good fortune; this is never the case with compulsive behaviour. Furthermore, obsessions can be distinguished from most superstitions in that the content of the obsession is often unacceptable or repugnant, leads to resistance, and causes distress. Obsessions also have a personal quality, whereas superstitions tend to be shared by many members of one's community or family. Superstitions in children are discussed in a later chapter (p. 104).

Distress and interference

What makes someone a candidate for the diagnosis of obsessive–compulsive disorder? The key question that needs to be asked is: Do the obsessions and/or compulsions cause him distress, or severely affect his functioning? If the problems are severe, they will undoubtedly cause much distress, and will interfere with his life. Experiencing an unwanted thought once a day on average could not conceivably cause someone any real distress, but if it were to happen dozens of times every hour, that would be distressing. Similarly, checking all the gas taps once or twice before leaving home hardly interferes with one's life, but if one were to check, say, seven times on each occasion, then that would certainly interfere with one's normal functioning. Some patients reach clinics or hospitals only after the problem has progressed to such a degree that it produces drastic effects on their lives. For example, a woman came for help only when her compulsions had developed to such an extent that she was spending all her waking hours cleaning the house. Another patient, a man, had resigned from his job because he became increasingly concerned with the germs that he thought would affect him through contact with others.

Sometimes the person's obsessions and compulsions are more distressing to others than to himself. Consider, for example, a man who had an obsessional concern about germs and dirt, and who carried out washing and cleaning rituals regularly. This might never have become a problem in itself, but he also began to insist that his wife and mother-in-law did the same. If they refused he would get very angry with them. He began to insist that they both wash their hands at certain times, that they keep their towels in certain places, and so on. The initial distress was thus felt not by him, but by others who were living with him.

In some, the compulsion is a minor one which does not affect one's life or functioning normally, but can be a problem in certain circumstances. A 26-year-old man had the compulsion to look at any stranger a second time. If he noticed someone on the street who went past him, he would immediately turn round and look at the person in question once again. This was a harmless, if peculiar, compulsion, and remained so until he acquired a girlfriend. The latter noticed this behaviour and immediately inferred that he was showing an unhealthy interest in other women, despite the fact that he was looking at members of both sexes indiscriminately! The ensuing dispute very nearly caused the break-up of their relationship. It was this that brought him to a psychologist for advice; otherwise he might never have felt any need to seek help. In another case, a man was accosted by store detectives in a large supermarket. He admitted that he had acted in a way that might have given rise to suspicion: he had a compulsion to touch with one hand anything that he had touched with the other, even if he had to turn round and go back to the object to do so, and to make the hand in question free by transferring whatever he was carrying to his other hand. Until this embarrassing event, he had not realized what a spectacle he was making of himself in public places.

What can we conclude from all this? Both obsessions and compulsions are common among people in the general population, and they are not considered as problems unless they cause distress or interfere with one's life. If, however, someone has obsessions and/or compulsions that cause him distress, or seriously affect his life activities, then he may need advice and help. It is this minority of people who are diagnosed as patients with obsessive–compulsive disorder.

The relationship between obsessions and compulsions

Thus far, obsessions and compulsions have been discussed as separate phenomena. What about the relationship between them? In some of the examples of compulsions given above, a relationship between the two is clearly implied. We referred, for instance, to a young woman who had the intrusive thought (obsession) that she might go blind whenever she saw black objects, which led to her engaging in the compulsive mental activity of visualizing objects of different colours (see p. 8). The relationship between the two events in this case is obvious: the obsession led to the compulsion. This is very common indeed; we know that, in the majority of cases of obsessive–compulsive disorder, obsessions and compulsions are related in this way. To give a common example, when someone gets the obsessional thought that he may have accidentally touched something that contaminated him, he is likely to feel a strong compulsive urge to decontaminate himself by washing his hands a certain number of times. These compulsions are sometimes described as 'neutralizing' behaviour, since they serve the function of neutralizing, or putting right, the preceding obsession or its feared consequences.

In a minority of cases, the obsession occurs by itself—that is, without leading to a compulsion. Here is an example:

> A young woman had recurrent thoughts and images of her wedding reception, which had taken place over a year ago. These thoughts centred mainly on the flower arrangements, which she felt had been unsatisfactory. The thoughts caused her discomfort, but there was no associated compulsion of any sort.

There are also cases, again a minority, where a compulsion takes place without a preceding obsession, as in this example:

> A man had a compulsion to imagine car registration plates in a certain way. Every time he noticed a car licence number plate, he compulsively visualized the same plate with the number transformed in certain specific ways, such as squared, halved, or multiplied by two.

Many people with extensive touching rituals do not report accompanying or preceding obsessions.

Elements of an obsessive–compulsive experience

One way to understand the relationship between obsessions and compulsions is to consider all the elements that may be present in an obsessive–compulsive experience (Table 3).

Table 3 Elements of an obsessive–compulsive experience

Trigger	External/internal/none
Obsession	Thought/image/impulse/none
Discomfort	+
Compulsive urge	+/−
Compulsive behaviour	Motor/cognitive/none
Discomfort reduction	+/−?
Fears of disaster	+/−
Inflated responsibility	+/−
Reassurance seeking	+/−
Avoidance	+/−
Disruption	External/internal/none

+ Indicates 'present'; − indicates 'absent'.

Trigger

A trigger is an event, or a cue, that sets off an obsession, a feeling or discomfort, or indeed a compulsive urge. A trigger may be external—that is, something in the environment—or internal. For example, a young woman had the obsession 'Did I stab someone?' or 'Will I stab my children?' every time she saw a knife or any other sharp object: the knife was the external trigger that provoked her obsession. Internal triggers are mental events that lead to the same result. A young man complained that, every time he remembered his deceased father, he experienced distressing obsessions about death. The memory of the father was the internal trigger for his obsessional thoughts. As indicated in Table 3, triggers are not invariably present in all obsessive–compulsive experiences.

Obsession

Since we have discussed obsessions in some detail already, we shall not dwell on this here. Suffice to say that there can be obsessive–compulsive experiences without an obsession as a part of them, although this is uncommon. A trigger—for example, seeing the walls of a room—may lead directly to a compulsive urge—for example, to touch them in a specific order.

Discomfort

The occurrence of the obsession usually leads to a feeling of discomfort. It may also, less commonly, be generated simply by exposure to the trigger, or by the compulsive urge. For many, this feeling is best described as anxiety, but some patients report that what they feel is not anxiety, but general unease, tension, or even a sense of guilt. 'Discomfort' is thus a better term to use here because it encompasses all these emotions. Note that Table 3 states that obsessive–compulsive experiences always include discomfort; however, this may not be so for non-clinical instances.

Compulsive urge

As noted above, this is the urge, or drive, that the person feels to carry out a particular behaviour, usually in a particular way. As Table 3 shows, not every obsessive–compulsive experience has this element.

Compulsive behaviour

This is the behaviour, overt or covert, that results from the compulsive urge. When the term 'compulsion' is used, it usually refers to the compulsive urge and the compulsive behaviour taken together.

Discomfort reduction

When the compulsive behaviour is carried out in the required manner, the patient normally feels relieved; the discomfort caused by the obsession (and/or the trigger, and/or the compulsive urge) is eliminated or reduced. In Table 3, we have also included a question mark against this element of obsessive–compulsive experience. This is because there are instances, admittedly few in number, where carrying out the compulsive behaviour does not lead to discomfort reduction. Indeed, in a small number of cases the discomfort may even increase. Moreover, even when the compulsive behaviour reduces the anxiety or discomfort, the person may be left feeling frustrated and demoralized.

Fears of disaster

These are found fairly frequently: the patient feels that a certain disaster will happen unless he wards it off by engaging in his compulsive behaviour. For example, an elderly man had the very strong fear that, if he did not check the gas taps in his house a certain number of times, the house would explode and go up in flames. The relationship between the specific disaster feared and the compulsive behaviour is, of course, not always logical. For example, a young man felt that his hand-washing rituals prevented major accidents occurring to his family members who lived in a different country. Similarly, patients who are troubled by obsessive fears, such as contracting AIDS, may wash excessively even though they know that washing your hands is irrelevant and ineffective as a precaution against AIDS.

Inflated responsibility

Many patients experience an inflated sense of responsibility—even for events over which they have no control. This is particularly common among those whose main problem is excessive checking. This inflated responsibility commonly generates intense guilt.

Most examples of compulsive checking are attempts to prevent a misfortune, however obscure. The person strives for certainty that no harm will occur to others because of his negligence or supposedly poor memory. 'I must check at least ten times to be absolutely sure that the stove is off and will not cause a deadly fire.' The drive to check repeatedly is intensified if and when the person feels solely or largely responsible for safety, for example if he is the last person to leave the house or office. Curiously, there is a tendency for affected people to believe that an accident or misfortune is definitely more likely to occur when they are responsible for the task than when someone else is responsible. This is one example of the so-called 'cognitive biases', or skewed reasoning, that sometimes occur in association with obsessive–compulsive disorder.

Inflated feelings of responsibility make a large contribution to obsessive–compulsive disorder. Hence, sufferers from obsessive–compulsive disorder may try to fend off responsibilities, for example by refusing promotions to more responsible positions, and are likely to be distressed if their responsibilities are increased. However, a reasoned and reasonable transfer of responsibility for therapeutic purposes can be a great relief.

Reassurance seeking

Many obsessive–compulsive patients resort to reassurance seeking, usually from members of their families. Often, obsessional thoughts such as 'Will I go insane?', 'Did I do it properly?', and 'Do I need to check the taps again?', lead to the patient asking for reassurance. When reassurance is received, the patient feels some relief from his discomfort. Reassurance seeking is often done repeatedly, much to the exasperation of friends and family. At best, the provision of such reassurance provides only brief relief.

Avoidance

This can be a significant factor in the clinical picture, although it is not part of the obsessive–compulsive experience itself. Usually, the avoidance behaviour concerns objects and situations that, potentially, can trigger the obsession or compulsion. For example, those with obsessions about dirt and germs, and associated washing or cleaning rituals, usually strive to avoid what they believe to be dirty or contaminating, and those with checking rituals may avoid situations that demand checking. Some patients with severe and extensive fears of contamination confine themselves to their bedroom; the rest of the world has to be avoided. A woman who had the obsessional thought that she might stab her children went to great lengths to avoid contact with knives, scissors, and other sharp objects. A young man who feared that he might catch AIDS, totally avoided certain areas of London. Sometimes, it is not places or things that are avoided, but behaviour. A patient may not wash in the morning, or at all, for several days because this behaviour requires a long and complicated ritual. An excellent example of avoidance of both objects and behaviour is as follows:

A married woman in her twenties had the obsessional thought that she had cancer. After several years of checking for cancer symptoms, she began to avoid any situation where she feared she might discover she had signs of cancer.

Thus, she would not make her bed in the morning, or look at her used underwear, for fear of discovering blood stains which, to her, would be a sign of the dreaded illness. She even stopped looking at herself in the mirror or at her own body. She began to wear blouses and jumpers with long sleeves so that she could not see her arms, and trousers so that she could not see her legs. She stopped washing herself properly, as she feared that she would discover lumps and such like on her body.

In some cases, certain numbers are avoided because the patient feels that such avoidance is needed in order to avert some disaster, usually to a loved one. An interesting illustration of this is found in the following example:

A young married woman began to avoid the number four. Her husband's birthday was on the fourth day of the month and her obsessional logic dictated that, if she did not avoid the number, she would cause great harm to him. She went to great lengths to achieve this; for instance, she would skip the fourth page of books and magazines she was reading, would never write the number four, never eat four of anything (e.g., potatoes or slices of bread), and so on. Life became impossible when this gradually extended to all numbers beginning or ending with four, multiples of four, those that are adjacent to four, and so on, at which point she sought help.

Disruption

When an obsessive–compulsive patient engages in his compulsion, he needs to carry it out precisely as he feels it ought to be done. If the behaviour is disrupted, then, for many, the compulsive ritual is invalidated and needs to be restarted. For long and complicated rituals this can be extremely time consuming and exhausting! The events that can act as disruptors vary from noise and other external disturbances to certain classes of experiences and thoughts.

A middle-aged man had recurrent, intrusive thoughts and images of past homosexual experiences. This led to feelings of guilt and distress. He had to 'cleanse his mind' with silent prayers to God uttered in a certain fixed sequence. If, during this praying, images of homosexual acts arose in his mind, then he had to restart the praying.

The need to form a safe or suitable thought before carrying out a compulsive or other act is common. If, as in the case described here, the action is disturbed by an unacceptable thought, the compulsive sequence has to be repeated in full.

> A young man engaged in prolonged hand-washing rituals whenever he felt his hands were contaminated by dirt and germs. He would usually wash them at the kitchen sink. If, during the activity, he happened to catch a glimpse of the kitchen waste bin, which he considered to be a dirty object, he felt his washing was not effective. So he would restart the washing ritual.

In some instances the person feels impelled to remove all other thoughts before attempting to carry out the compulsive activity; for example, removing distracting thoughts all the better to concentrate on making sure that you have checked the stove correctly.

Other key terms

Two other key terms, which are commonly used to describe aspects of obsessive–compulsive disorder, need explanation. They are 'ritual' and 'rumination'.

What is a ritual?

A ritual, in the context of obsessive–compulsive disorder, is a compulsive behaviour, either overt or mental; it implies that the behaviour concerned has a rigid, set pattern and a sequence of steps with a clear-cut beginning and end. Some examples of compulsive behaviour are highly ritualized. The following example illustrates a very elaborate ritual reported by a man in his mid-twenties. This is what he had to do when brushing his teeth and washing his face every morning.

> Enter bathroom with left foot first.
>
> Close door with left hand, then touch door handle with right hand.
>
> Take towel from rail and keep it on edge of bath with left hand, then touch it with right hand.
>
> Take toothbrush from cabinet and place it on edge of washbasin with left hand, then touch it with right hand.
>
> Take toothpaste tube from cabinet with left hand, then touch it with right hand.
>
> Unscrew and remove cap with left hand, then touch it with right hand.

Squeeze tube to get enough toothpaste on to brush with left hand, then touch tube with right hand.

Replace cap of tube with left hand, then touch it with right hand.

Put tube back with left hand, then touch it with right hand.

Pick up brush with left hand, then start brushing: teeth brushed in twos, from left to right, top row first, bottom row next, outside first, inside next, each set of two eight times; then, repeat whole process with brush in right hand, then again with left hand followed by same again with right hand.

Open taps with left hand, then touch them with right hand.

Wash brush under hot tap, held in left hand, then touch it with right hand.

Put brush back in cabinet with left hand, then touch it with right hand.

Rinse mouth, taking water with left hand, then with right hand.

Look at self in mirror first with left eye, then with right eye.

Begin to wash face, using left hand to splash water on face, then right hand.

Rub left side of face with left hand, followed by right side of face with left hand, then rub left side of face with right hand, followed by right side of face with right hand.

Apply soap to face, in the same sequence as above.

Rinse face, splashing water on face with left hand, then with right hand.

Look at self in the mirror, first with left eye, them with right eye.

Close taps with left hand, then touch them with right hand.

Pick up towel with left hand, then touch it with right hand.

Dry face with towel, left side holding towel in left hand, then right side holding towel in left hand, then left side holding towel in right hand, then right side holding towel in right hand.

Look at self in mirror, first with left eye, then with right eye.

Put towel back on rail with left hand, then touch it with right hand.

Open door with left hand, then touch handle with right hand.

Leave bathroom, with left foot first.

Most compulsive behaviour has a ritualistic quality about it, and for this reason the term 'ritual' is used by many to refer to any compulsive behaviour;

in this book, the word 'ritual' is used in this broad sense. Similarly, engaging in compulsive behaviour is sometimes referred to as 'ritualizing'.

What are ruminations?

A rumination is a train of thought, unproductive and prolonged, on a particular topic or theme. Some authors and clinicians use the term 'obsessional rumination' to refer to all obsessional thoughts, but this is misleading. An example of a rumination is as follows:

> A young man had complicated and time-consuming rumination on the question: 'Is everyone basically good?' He would ruminate on this for a long time, going over in his mind various considerations and arguments and contemplating what superficially appeared to him to be relevant evidence. This never led to a solution or satisfactory conclusion.

How does a rumination differ from an obsession? Unlike obsessions, ruminations do not intrude into the patient's consciousness, in a well-defined form, or with a clearly circumscribed content. Clinically, it appears that ruminations are mental compulsive behaviour, usually preceded by an obsession. For example, the obsession 'Am I going mad?' may lead to the compulsive urge to think through the subject, which in turn leads to a muddled attempt at thinking about it; this is the rumination. Ruminations are different from other mental compulsions in that the latter consist of specific mental acts, such as saying something silently or visualizing something in a particular way (see examples on p. 8). Ruminations are not such well-defined events; the theme or topic of a rumination is specific, but what goes into the thinking about the topic is open-ended and variable.

Many ruminations of obsessive–compulsive patients tend to concern religious, philosophical, or metaphysical subjects such as the origins of the universe, life after death, the nature of morality, and so on.

> One young man reported extensive ruminations about what would happen to him after death. He would weigh up the various theoretical possibilities, visualize scenes of heaven, hell, and other worlds, try to remember what philosophers and scientists have said about death, and so on. There was never a satisfying end-point. A cycle of rumination, he reported, would take well over an hour.

The case of a young man, a student who had mathematical ruminations, has been described recently by Drs Idit Albert and Peter Hayward of the University of London. While studying or listening to lectures in class, he would get the thought that he was not understanding the subject adequately. This would then lead to thoughts such as, 'What is the difference between a vector and a point in space?' He would then ruminate on these questions. This had the effect of making his studying time much longer. These ruminations also left him feeling low. Drs Albert and Hayward have characterized this young man's difficulty as feeling compelled to worry about problems that he knew he could never resolve.

2
Relationship to other disorders

In this chapter, we shall discuss the relationship between obsessive–compulsive disorder and some other psychological disorders.

Depression

There is a clear relationship between obsessive–compulsive disorder and depression. This can take several forms. First, some people develop obsessions when they become depressed; in such cases the obsessions are essentially secondary to the depression, and usually clear up when the depression lifts. It has been observed that, among obsessions developing in the context of a depressive illness, about half have a content of aggression of a homicidal or suicidal nature, whereas among obsessive–compulsive patients such content is found much less often. Secondly, many obsessive–compulsive patients tend to have a past history of episodes of depression. Thirdly, some of these patients become depressed subsequent to the onset of their disorder, and may have episodes of depression. When depressed, the symptoms of obsessive–compulsive disorder tend to get worse. Research has also shown that if the patient is very depressed he may not respond well to the standard psychological treatment of the obsessive–compulsive disorder. In such cases, the depression needs to be treated before improvement can be expected in the obsessive–compulsive symptoms.

In view of the relationship between the two disorders, a word is necessary about the features of depression. The major features are: seriously depressed mood; loss of interest or pleasure in usual activities; disturbance of appetite and sleep; severe slowing or agitation; feelings of worthlessness or extreme guilt; extensive pessimism; and suicidal ideas.

Morbid preoccupations

Morbid preoccupations are often found in depressed patients, and sometimes in normal people during phases of low mood. There is some similarity and overlap between obsessions and morbid preoccupations: both consist of intrusive and repetitive ideas. However, preoccupations differ in significant ways from true obsessions in that they centre on realistic current problems or worries, and lack the repugnant or nonsensical quality of obsessions. They are rarely resisted, and the person usually recognizes them to be rational, if exaggerated.

Schizophrenia

The relationship with schizophrenia is more limited. In schizophrenia, stereotyped behaviour, which may appear like compulsive behaviour, is sometimes evident. It is also known that, in the early stages of schizophrenic illness, obsessions and compulsions may appear occasionally, but these are short-lived. Complaints of schizophrenic patients about thoughts that they wished they did not have can bear a superficial similarity to obsessions, but these are usually thoughts that they believe to have been put into their minds by external forces, human or otherwise. This feature clearly distinguishes them from obsessional thoughts, which the patient recognizes as his own.

Many years ago, some writers and clinicians held the view that obsessive–compulsive disorder and schizophrenia were closely related conditions. The medical literature of the nineteenth century suggested that obsessive–compulsive disorder was a variant of schizophrenia, and it was classified at that time within the spectrum of psychotic disorders. Some authors even took the view that the disorder is a defence against a schizophrenic breakdown. There is no evidence to support this view, and the belief in a connection with schizophrenia is discredited. The chances of an obsessive–compulsive patient developing schizophrenia subsequently are no higher than those of any other person.

However, obsessive–compulsive patients are sometimes diagnosed (or misdiagnosed) as schizophrenic. This is largely because of the superficial similarity between obsessions and the delusions (intensely held, personal, false beliefs) that patients with schizophrenia commonly hold. Ordinarily, the two phenomena can be distinguished from each other. A schizophrenic delusion is a belief intensely held by the patient—that is, he has no insight that it is false (e.g., he *really* believes that his enemies are sending radio waves to harm him), whereas an obsession is experienced as ego-dystonic—that is, not in keeping with one's own beliefs and thoughts—and is seen as unwanted. In other words, the obsessive–compulsive patient has insight;

he knows that his obsessional belief—for example, that some disaster is about to happen to his loved ones—is really not valid. Although the patient acts on the belief by performing compulsive behaviour or avoiding certain things, there is the recognition, if not at the time of the behaviour then a few hours later, that it is ultimately irrational. Admittedly there are exceptions, but they are very small in number. The American Psychiatric Association, in its most recent guidelines on obsessive–compulsive disorder, refers to those 'with poor insight'. These are patients who, for most of the time during the current episode of the disorder, do not recognize that their obsessions or compulsions are irrational or excessive. In this minority of patients, the obsessional belief is held with some tenacity. In recent years, some writers have commented on such strongly held beliefs in obsessive–compulsive patients and described them as 'overvalued ideas'. Despite the strength of these delusion-like beliefs, many of these patients can ultimately be persuaded to concede that they may be mistaken.

Phobias

Sometimes obsessive–compulsive disorders are confused with phobias, which are irrational and/or excessive fears. In view of their common features, this is not surprising. Phobias are characterized by anxiety, and most obsessive–compulsive patients experience a lot of anxiety. As noted earlier (see Table 1, p. 2), both conditions fall within the category of anxiety disorders. In both, there is avoidance behaviour: a patient with a phobia of spiders will avoid going near them or to places where he knows spiders are to be found; an obsessive–compulsive patient with a concern about dirt will avoid all places and objects that he thinks contain dirt. It is certainly the case that some obsessive–compulsive patients have some phobic characteristics, particularly those with contamination fears and related washing and cleaning rituals.

However, the two disorders are different in some important ways. The ritualistic behaviour of the obsessive–compulsive patient is absent in the phobic. Many of the former may describe their feeling, when affected by an obsession or exposed to a triggering situation such as contact with dirt, not so much as 'fear' but as 'discomfort', 'uneasiness', or 'disgust'. A further important difference is that someone with a phobia usually can, if he successfully avoids the object or situation he is afraid of, feel safe and be unaffected by the problem in his day-to-day life. Someone with a phobia of elevators, for example, will avoid using elevators and will be able to lead a perfectly happy life as long as he is not forced to use an elevator, and someone with a phobia of spiders can lead a normal life as long as he avoids encounters with spiders. In contrast, an obsessive–compulsive patient cannot escape from his problems as easily; even if he keeps away from things that trigger his obsessions or compulsive urges, he does not feel free. For example, a woman with this disorder may totally avoid knives, scissors, and other sharp objects, which she fears she may use to attack people, but will still frequently worry that she may commit these acts, or indeed even wonder whether she has actually attacked someone.

So, despite some similarities and overlap, obsessive–compulsive disorder and phobic disorder are different from each other.

Eating disorders

Anorexia nervosa

Anorexia nervosa has been described by some writers as a form of obsessive–compulsive disorder. The single-minded determination to lose weight and the incessant preoccupation with food, weight, and body size and shape that these patients display have been given as evidence for this. Anorexics are commonly described as 'obsessed with thinness'. They are certainly preoccupied with their weight, size, and eating. However, anorexia nervosa is a separate disorder, not part of an obsessive–compulsive illness, although there is some relationship between the two, and a small proportion of females with obsessive–compulsive disorder have a past history of anorexia nervosa. Among anorexics, a sizeable subgroup has obsessions and/or compulsions, some of them quite marked. It appears that, in these patients, the two disorders coexist. In fact many studies have reported this co-morbidity in a significant minority of anorexic patients. Sometimes, the symptoms of the two disorders influence each other and get intertwined—that is, certain behaviour assumes significance in both disorders. For example, an adolescent girl had the compulsive behaviour of running up and down the stairs a certain number of times before every meal. This had all the features of a compulsion, but it could equally be seen as anorexic behaviour, designed to lose weight—and it certainly had that effect. She also had the compulsion to leave a quantity of food on her plate, arranged in a certain way, unconsumed. Her explanation was that she felt compelled to do this. Although she denied that it had anything to do with eating less, the behaviour clearly contributed to maintaining a lower weight.

Patients with both anorexia and obsessive–compulsive problems report that their latter difficulties tend to get worse when they are particularly unhappy with their weight and body size. It is also known that anorexics with obsessive–compulsive symptoms tend to display more severe anorexic disorders than those who do not have such symptoms.

Bulimia nervosa

In bulimia nervosa the patient has recurrent episodes of binge eating, followed by self-induced vomiting and/or laxative abuse. The urge to engage in binge eating is described by some of these patients as having a compulsive quality, although the nature of the behaviour is by no means senseless. As with anorexics, some bulimics also have concomitant obsessive–compulsive problems, some features of which may become closely related to the eating disorder. For example, a young woman with a history of both disorders reported that when she binged on chocolate bars she felt compelled to eat twenty-four bars at a time, neither more nor fewer, and the binge had to be uninterrupted. If the chocolates got 'contaminated' by the smell of another food, then the binging episode had to be restarted.

Post-traumatic stress disorder

Post-traumatic stress disorder is another of the anxiety disorders (see Table 1, p. 2). The psychological effects of severe traumatic experiences have been known and recorded for a long time, but it is only in recent years that the diagnostic category of 'post-traumatic stress disorder' has been recognized officially. Essentially, this refers to a psychological disorder that some people develop after exposure to a traumatic event (e.g., war, earthquakes and fires, violence, serious motor accidents). The main features are the persistent re-experiencing of the traumatic event—for example, recurrent intrusive memories, recurrent dreams; avoidance of reminders of the event; and increased arousal, as reflected by sleep difficulties, poor concentration, and so on. Large numbers of war veterans have been treated for this disorder in the United States and elsewhere, and there is an active and still growing interest in this area.

The recurrent, intrusive thoughts and images that occur in this disorder are very much like some of the obsessions experienced by patients with obsessive–compulsive disorder. This is particularly so for the very vivid intrusive images. For example, a former soldier now suffering from post-traumatic stress disorder had the recurrent image of bloated and charred bodies. It is also not uncommon for sufferers to have intrusive thoughts other than memories of the event (e.g. 'Why did it have to happen to me?' 'Am I really safe now?'). Some also report cognitive compulsions, such as compulsively saying 'No, it wasn't my fault', or compulsively going over the incident, step by step, in great detail.

In a small number of patients with this disorder, overt compulsive rituals are found. One, a 46-year-old man who was subjected to a particularly vicious act of violence, developed rituals of repeatedly checking door and window locks. A young woman who was seriously sexually assaulted while on holiday, began to wash herself compulsively in order to 'become clean'.

While the overlap of some of the features of obsessive–compulsive disorder and post-traumatic disorder is clear, are the two related? There are certainly instances in which a trauma victim has developed obsessions and/or compulsions, to the degree that one can describe him as suffering from obsessive–compulsive disorder. It is also clear that a small number of obsessive–compulsive patients have a history of traumatic or disturbing experiences. However, the two disorders are different entities, and the majority of patients with obsessive–compulsive disorder do not have a history of trauma. Similarly, the majority of patients who suffer from post-traumatic disorder do not develop full-blown obsessive–compulsive disorder. A small number do, and may have both disorders concurrently. In some, the obsessive–compulsive disorder remains even after the full-blown post-traumatic disorder has resolved.

A married woman in her forties had a horrendous car accident. The car suddenly blew a tyre on a busy road, and when it stopped it was hit by a vehicle coming rather fast from behind. The car went up in flames, and a young child—a friend's son—strapped to a seat, perished. She developed severe post-traumatic stress disorder, with recurrent intrusive images and other symptoms. She began to ask her husband for reassurance, especially about the safety of their own child, and would check the child's bedroom at night several times. She also had the compulsion to visualize the child who died, in bright clothes and smiling. She was quite guilt-ridden and depressed. She later developed a range of general checking and cleaning rituals. When seen eighteen months after the accident, she had full-blown obsessive–compulsive disorder.

Gilles de la Tourette syndrome

This condition is characterized by multiple tics, including vocal tics which may take the form of swear words or obscenities. These tics are different from true compulsions—they are purposeless and involuntary, unlike compulsions. Nor can they be easily delayed, reshaped or substituted, again unlike compulsions. Another difference is that the treatment methods that are successful with obsessive–compulsive disorder are of little use with Tourette patients.

It has been reported that some patients with this syndrome also have obsessive–compulsive symptoms, particularly the younger patients. In some studies, first-degree relatives of Tourette patients have also been reported to have a higher incidence of obsessive–compulsive disorder than the general population. However, despite these apparent associations, the vast majority of patients with obsessive–compulsive disorder do not have Gilles de la Tourette syndrome.

Body dysmorphic disorder

The disorder, which used to be called 'dysmorphophobia', is character-ized by excessive concern and preoccupation with imagined defects in bodily appearance. The common complaints are about the face or head (e.g., shape or size of nose, mouth, eyebrows, chin, or jaws). Less com-monly, the person may be over-concerned with some other part of the body (such as hands, feet, breasts, or genitals). Asymmetry or lack of pro-portion can also be a concern. In some cases, cosmetic surgery is sought. The repetitive thoughts in this disorder may resemble obsessions, and the person usually engages in extensive checking behaviour, especially in the mirror. Reassurance seeking is also common. In some cases, the conviction that there is a physical abnormality leads to social avoidance.

Despite the repetitive thoughts and checking, body dysmorphic disorder is quite distinct from obsessive–compulsive disorder. It is not considered to be an anxiety disorder at all. However, a small percentage of patients with body dysmorphic disorder also have co-morbid obsessive–compulsive disorder.

Brain damage

Symptoms similar to obsessions and compulsions can result from brain damage caused by injury or neurological disease: the patient may engage in repetitive acts or express repetitive ideas. The appearance of obsessive–compulsive-type symptoms in certain organic conditions (e.g., encephalitis lethargica) has been recognized for many decades. These symptoms are usually accompanied by other signs of brain damage, such as deficits in memory and learning ability. Furthermore, repetitive acts and ideas of these patients are different from obsessions and compulsions in that they lack intellectual content and intentionality, and have a mechanical or prim-itive quality. Studies undertaken to investigate the neurological and neu-ropsychological features of obsessive–compulsive patients have not, up to now, produced consistent or clear-cut results. It is safe to say that there is no evidence of any brain damage in the vast majority of obsessive–compulsive patients.

Obsessional personality

Different views have been expressed on the relationship between obsessive–compulsive disorder and obsessional personality (also called 'compulsive personality' and 'anankastic personality'). By obsessional personality we mean a group of enduring characteristics in a person, including orderliness, meticulousness, preoccupation with detail, parsimony, obstinacy, neatness, difficulty handling uncertainty, and perfectionism. According to some writers, obsessive–compulsive disorder is only an exaggerated stage or version of an obsessional personality. This is incorrect: obsessional personality traits are acceptable to the person, seldom cause distress, and are rarely accompanied by a sense of compulsion. They rarely provoke resistance. Perhaps even more importantly, these personality traits show much greater stability than obsessive–compulsive disorder.

A related view is that the premorbid personality—i.e. the personality before the onset of the disorder—of obsessive–compulsive patients is of the obsessional type. However, this is not supported by satisfactory evidence. It is true that a proportion of obsessive–compulsive patients do have an obsessional-type personality, but many more with very different personality features also develop the disorder. Conversely, the great majority of persons with obsessional personalities never develop obsessive–compulsive disorder.

If we were to look for any single personality type that is associated with the disorder, it would perhaps best be described as cautious and introverted, rather than obsessional. Even this has to be seen as only a very general observation, for there are numerous exceptions.

Obsessive–compulsive personality disorder

Persons with obsessional personality features, to a degree that seriously affects their life and functioning, are sometimes clinically described as suffering from an obsessive–compulsive personality disorder, also called 'obsessional personality disorder' or 'compulsive personality disorder'. In these patients, the main features are long-standing personality traits such as excessive rigidity and perfectionism, undue preoccupation with details, indecisiveness, and so on, and not episodes of illness. These features are well established by early adulthood, and they are present in a variety of contexts. In addition, these people tend to show a lack of, or limited ability to express, warm and tender emotions. They do not necessarily have, or develop, true obsessions and compulsions. In clinical practice, such patients are encountered only rarely and, when they do come for help, it is usually because of a depressive or other illness. It has been observed that this disorder is more common in males than females. Sometimes a patient may display features of this disorder as well as obsessive–compulsive disorder. In such cases a dual diagnosis is given.

Obsessive–compulsive personality disorder is not classified under anxiety disorders. It is, essentially a personality disorder, and has little in common with anxiety disorders.

3
Obsessive–compulsive patients

There are several common forms of obsessive–compulsive disorder. Most patients have more than one problem, but usually there are one or two that are predominant at a given time. At the time of coming for help, many also display general anxiety, low mood, frustration, and considerable overall distress.

Main clinical types

These can be categorized as:

1. those with washing/cleaning compulsions as the major problem;
2. those with checking compulsions as the major problem;
3. those with other overt compulsions as the major problem;
4. those with compulsive hoarding;
5. those with obsessions unaccompanied by overt compulsive behaviour;
6. those with primary obsessional slowness.

Washers/cleaners

This is the most common clinical presentation. Typically, the patient has obsessions about contamination by dirt or germs, or pollution from something more specific, like urine, faeces, seminal fluid, animal fur, asbestos, and so on, and related washing and cleaning rituals. There is also avoidance, in an attempt to keep away from contact with dirt or other sources of contamination or pollution. The washing and cleaning can be severely excessive; in some cases this involves washing one's hands over a hundred times a day, using bottles of detergent, using hundreds of toilet papers, bathing or showering for several hours, washing and wiping table tops, chairs, and floors for much of the day, and so on. The reasons given for the washing or cleaning are varied. Often, it is for the purpose of getting rid of dirt or germs. This is linked, in some, to ensuring that a serious illness (such as cancer or AIDS) is not contracted. In some cases, the cleaning is aimed at protecting others from the spread of germs. A few say that they have to engage in the washing and cleaning ritual simply to avert the great anxiety, even panic, that would occur if it was not done properly.

The avoidance can be extensive. The patient may avoid objects that others have touched, such as door knobs and public telephones; he may refrain from using public toilets, and avoid sitting on chairs that others have sat on, or—if he did—would first cover it with a towel or cloth or sit on the edge. In severe cases, the entire world, except a small area in one's home, is avoided. One woman was so concerned about dirt and germs that she felt free only in her bedroom and the bathroom, which she did not allow anyone else to enter. When she went out she wore a large coat and gloves, which she immediately washed upon returning. All items brought into the bedroom had to be cleaned or washed first. Another patient felt some safety only when sitting in her exclusive chair at home; she disinfected her chair daily (see below).

There is an excess of females over males among those whose main problem is washing/cleaning.

The following is a case illustration:

A young woman had obsessions about dirt, and related compulsions. Her main concern was about excrement, both human and animal. She would wash extensively after returning from a walk even if she did not actually see, let alone step on, dirt. This was because she felt that dog dirt is spread all over the roads and pavements by rain and wind. She would leave her shoes outside the door and change into a different pair before entering the house. She totally avoided public toilets. As the problem got worse, she began to avoid going anywhere near manholes because they indicated the presence of sewers with human excreta underneath. She would avoid parts of roads in her area where she knew there were manholes. By the time she came for help, she had almost wholly stopped going out, and left her job as a result, and had begun to spend much of her time in bed. She had also begun to demand that her parents, with whom she lived, stop going out, as they would bring dirt into the house when they returned, and to insist that they left their shoes outside and washed their hands and feet when they returned from an outing.

Here is another example:

> A married woman in her mid-thirties developed a severe and pervasive fear of contracting cancer through contact with any person, or with things that had come close to a person, with the disease. She recognized that her fear was scientifically groundless but, despite this, it was intense. In order to reduce the chances of contracting cancer, she spent hours each day washing, cleaning, and disinfecting herself and her clothes. She did not feel safe going out, so did not leave her house except for the most urgent of reasons. She felt more secure in one room of the house, and on one chair in particular, which she disinfected every day. Her hands were red, swollen, and abraded, due to excessive washing.

The hands of many compulsive hand washers show clear signs of excessive washing. The repeated washing tends to dry the natural oils in the skin and frequently causes marked dryness, especially in the areas between the fingers.

Fear of dirt and germs—a patient's account

The following is a female patient's own account of her washing and cleaning compulsions. She was in her fifties, and lived on her own in an apartment.

> I cannot touch anything that I think is dirty. It is mainly the toilet, but then when you come out of the toilet you bring the dirt and the germs out into other parts of the house. I always wash my hands many times before I leave the toilet. I keep my shoes and slippers outside the door of the toilet, so I can step into them as I come out. No, I would never use a public toilet, never. I nearly died when once a young man who came in to fix something used my toilet. He just came out and went on touching things, walking about the place, as if everything was fine! I couldn't tell him to stop, but it was so *awful*. I cleaned and cleaned all over the house after he left. I used disinfectant on the things he touched, even the things he went near. I don't like people coming into my home, not even friends, any more. My bedroom I somehow keep clean. Every other part of the house is really dirty, however much I clean. The towels I have in the toilet I wash separately, never with my other things. When I feel I am dirty I wash and wash, with lots of soap, and with Dettol and whatnot. The whole house smells of disinfectant. I feel fine for a while when I have washed but, when I go to the toilet again, even to pick up something or to open the window, it starts all over again. I don't think I can allow myself to be touched by anyone. I keep my gloves on when I am in shops or on the bus. All the clothes I wear for outside, I never bring into the bedroom without first washing them. If the bedroom also got dirty then I would be finished. Where could I go? That is the only clean place which I have.

The germ war of Howard Hughes

It is well know that the late American millionaire Howard Hughes (1905–76) had severe contamination obsessions and related rituals and avoidance behaviour, particularly in the later years of his life. Among other things, he had complicated rituals for handling objects. For example, before handing a spoon to Hughes, his attendants were required to wrap its handle in tissue paper and seal it with cellophane tape. A second piece of tissue paper was then wrapped over the first protective wrapping. On receiving the spoon, Hughes would use it with the handle still covered. He gave even more detailed instructions for many other activities, all related to his great fear of germs and contamination, and his staff had to adhere to these instructions very strictly. Typical of these were his instructions on how to remove his hearing aid cord from the bathroom cabinet. First, six to eight Kleenex tissues had to be used for touching the door knob to open the bathroom door. Then the taps were to be opened, using the same tissues, to obtain warm water. Next, six to eight Kleenex tissues were to be used to open the cabinet that contained the soap, and an unused bar of soap taken. The hands were then to be washed thoroughly, making sure that they did not touch the taps or the sides of the bowl. Next, fifteen to twenty new Kleenex tissues had to be used to turn off the taps. Now the door of the cabinet that contained the hearing aid cord was to be opened, using at least fifteen Kleenexes. Nothing inside the cabinet was to be touched in any way, except the sealed envelope that contained the cord. This was to be removed with both hands, using at least 15 Kleenexes for each hand. Only the centres of the tissues were to be allowed to come into contact with the envelope.

On those occasions when his staff had to touch him in order to wake him up, Hughes's instructions were that the chosen person should pinch his toes with eight thicknesses of Kleenex tissues, applying progressively greater pressure until he woke up.

Checkers

Those with checking compulsions form the next largest clinical group of obsessive–compulsives. Males and females are found in roughly equal numbers in this group. These patients engage in excessive checking rituals. A typical checker will repeatedly check things such as gas taps, ovens, electrical appliances and switches, door locks, windows, cupboards, drawers, cabinets, or files. The checking is associated with obsessions that take the form of doubting, such as 'Did I switch off the gas?', 'I may have left the oven on', 'The door must have been left unlocked', and so on.

Checkers worry a great deal over these doubts until they check and recheck. Checking once is not enough; often it is many times (not infrequently a fixed number of times) and even then some patients may feel vaguely unhappy. The checking takes time, it can be very embarrassing if others notice it, and it can be disabling. One young woman was not able to park her car and leave it until she had checked all the switches, radio, aerial, and all doors and windows several times. She would walk around the car, looking and checking, before leaving it. Some patients drive back home when they are halfway to work, to check their gas taps, light switches, and door locks.

Most checkers strive to make sure that they have not left any chance of harm coming to themselves or others. Their fear is that there will be disasters if they do not ensure that whatever they are worried about is properly checked. The underlying motive in most compulsive checking is the fear of being responsible for harm coming to other people. A strong sense of inflated responsibility is commonly associated with compulsive checking. A middle-aged plumber had to check and recheck every plumbing job he had done, however small. If he did not do this, he felt that the pipes would burst and the building would be flooded. He sometimes invented excuses to return to houses where he had done a job, in order to do his checking. In some cases, the disasters feared are remote, and not in anyway connected to the behaviour—such as air crashes involving relatives, or even earthquakes.

While many checkers are worried about things like doors and gas taps, which many people will check (though not excessively), some checkers have less easily understood concerns. A patient may check every chair for pins or sharp objects, or for pieces of glass. For example, a young man compulsively checked every garbage bag that he walked past to make sure that it contained just rubbish, and not a corpse. Another man repeatedly drove back along the way he had just gone, to check if he had knocked down a pedestrian or an animal. Retracing one's path or journey is a relatively common form of compulsive checking.

The following is a case example of a checker:

A man in his late twenties was referred with extensive checking behaviour. He felt compelled to check that 'everything was right', so he would go back over everything he did. The most serious doubts he had were about doors, windows, and gas taps, which he checked several times before leaving the house in the morning and before retiring to bed at night. He also checked anything that he wrote several times, which delayed his work considerably. He could not put anything in an envelope or a file, drawer, or cabinet without repeatedly checking that he had written exactly the right thing. He often ripped opened sealed envelopes to reread what he had written. He also checked the dates of newspapers: while reading a newspaper, he would check repeatedly that it was that day's, even if it had just been delivered to him. Some of his checking, he felt, was necessary to avoid fires, the house being burgled, the bathroom getting flooded, and so on. For the rest, he had only a vague notion that it was necessary to avoid some unspecified calamity. At the time that he came for help, he was seriously affected by the problem; nothing could be left unchecked, and his work was becoming impossible.

The patients in all of these examples had an exaggerated sense of responsibility and felt that it was incumbent upon them to prevent errors or disasters from taking place. To this end, they felt compelled to carry out their checking rituals. When the feeling of responsibility of such patients is transferred or suspended, the compulsive checking tends to decline or even stop altogether. So, for example, a woman who carried out repeated checks of the light switches, gas taps, and so on in her own house, is free of these compulsions when visiting the house of others. If these people are admitted to hospital for in-patient treatment, they typically show little or no checking behaviour in the first few days. As they settle in, however, they begin to feel responsible for the security of the ward and then their checking re-emerges.

An illuminating account of compulsive checking has been given by Frederick Toates, a British experimental psychologist, who has written about the obsessive–compulsive problems he suffered. He checked and double-checked that he had switched off electrical equipment, locked doors, etc. He could not resist going back to yet one more 'final' check. He has described how he had to go back three kilometres to his laboratory one night to check that all the equipment had been properly switched off. This was despite the fact that he had already checked twice, before leaving the laboratory, that everything was switched off. Dr Toates also checked the contents of letters. After writing and sealing letters and taking them to the post, he would feel unsure that he had put the right letter in the right envelope; so he would tear them open and read their contents again.

Those with other overt compulsions

There are some whose main problem consists of compulsions that do not fall into the above categories. There is no preponderance of either males or females in this heterogeneous group. Some repeat certain behaviour, such as getting dressed or undressed several times. One young woman had the compulsion to go back into the bathroom three times after a bath or wash, before she could go on to other things. Some have to do things in a certain way—for example, a strict sequence has to be followed in preparing a meal or setting the table (see pp. 20–21 for an example of an elaborate ritual of this type). Each step is rigidly predetermined in terms of its place in the sequence of behaviour. Some have touching compulsions—touching corners of a room, touching with one hand what has been touched with the other, and ensuring equal contact time for each hand, are examples. Some of the behaviour appears bizarre to others, and patients may try to conceal the compulsive behaviour.

The reason given by many patients for doing these things is usually the same as that given by checkers: if they do not do it, some danger or harm would happen, usually to a loved one. In some the reason is very specific, while in others it can be a vague feeling of harm or danger. For a small number of patients the compulsion is not a way of warding off any harm. They say they just have to do it because, if they did not, the feeling of discomfort or anxiety would be too great to bear.

Another interesting compulsion is list-making. The patient makes a list—of things to do, things to buy, people to telephone, and so on—well beyond the bounds of reason. One young woman had to make a detailed list each morning of every single thing that she had to do during the day, including such simple routine things as having breakfast, going to the toilet, putting on shoes, and so on. When each behaviour was completed, it was crossed off the list. Items not on the list could not be performed. This behaviour was so time-consuming that she was late for everything. When her mother once took away her notebook, she began to write on the palms of her hands.

Other overt compulsions include completing things, arranging things in symmetrical order or in some other regular way, straightening things, looking at things in a certain way, or looking at particular things, colours, and so on. Another quite common variant centres on serious discomfort arising when interrupted by unwanted intrusions. For example, while making tea, one may hear the word 'death' or 'murder' on the radio, or happen to see a 'dirty' object like a waste bin, which may necessitate the whole operation being started afresh. This is repeated until a 'clear run' is achieved. Sometimes the person feels compelled to achieve a 'clear head' even before starting to arrange, straighten, or settle objects. The type of event that can disrupt a behaviour and necessitate a repetition is usually something to do with dirt, danger, illness, and so on, but it can also be something of personal relevance (such as hearing the name of a loved one) or a senseless triviality (e.g., hearing words beginning with 'z').

A patient's account of her day

The following is a patient's own account of the form of compulsion described in this section. She was 20 years old and was in hospital for another problem at the time that she wrote this account of a day as an in-patient. As can be seen, 'number rituals' dominated her life. Her problems had started when she was 9.

During the course of the night, I get in and out of the bed four times.

7 a.m. I get out of bed for the fourth time, put my contact lenses in and take them out four times, then make my bed, folding each corner four times, straightening the blankets and tucking them in four times, arranging the pillows four times, pulling the bed away from the wall and pushing it back in place four times, folding and unfolding the extra blankets four times, straightening the top cover four times, and drawing the curtains back and forth four times. I go to the toilet, put the lid of the toilet down and lift it up again four times, wash my hands four times, and go to the lounge counting my steps in fours in my head. I look at each corner of the room four times, counting the chairs in the room four times, and go back to the dormitory counting four times. I then pick up my washbag and put it down four times, go to the washroom counting in fours, pull the curtain back and forth four times, wash each part of my body four times, clean my contact lenses four times, brush my teeth and hair four times, and go back to the dormitory counting in fours.

8 a.m. Breakfast—I pull my chair in at the table four times, recite in my head four different prayers four times, use the pepper four times, putting it on four different places on my plate, put my knife and fork down four times during the meal, chew the food four times or in multiples of four, and use four teaspoons of coffee, stirring it four times. I get up from the table and go to the lounge counting in fours, get up and sit down four times, say four different prayers four times, touch each corner of the chair four times. I now shower—I step in and out of the shower four times, switch the water on and off four times, wash each part of my body four times, shampoo my hair four times, rinse my hair and flannel four times, dry each part of my body four times, put my nightdress on and take it off four times. After cleaning out each drawer of my bedside locker four times, I fold up the clothes in my wardrobe four times, change the water in the flower vase four times, dry my hair with the hair-dryer while counting in fours, put my washing into the washing machine and take it out four times, switch the machine on and off four times, and tidy the toiletries on my locker while counting in fours, picking each item up and putting it down four times. I go to the telephone counting in fours, pick up the receiver and put it down four times before dialling, look at the dial four times, and put the receiver down and pick it up four times at the end of the conversation. After going back to the washroom counting in fours, I pull the curtains back and forth four times, go to the toilet, put down the lid and lift it up four times, wash my hands and clean my contact lenses four times, blow my nose four times, and recite in my head four different prayers four times.

Noon Lunch—I pull my chair in at the table four times, look at each person at the table four times before each course, cut each piece of food into four pieces or multiples of four, chew each piece of food four times, and swallow, counting in fours. I wipe my hands on my flannel four times, then go to the lounge counting my steps in fours, sit down and stand up four times, take my slippers off and put them back on four times, touch each corner of the chair four times, look at each corner of the room four times, look at each person in the room four times.

6 p.m. Supper—I pull my chair in at the table four times, look at each person at the table four times, and use the pepper four times.

10 p.m. I queue up for medication and count each person in the queue four times, go through to the washroom counting my steps in fours, wash each part of my body four times, brush my teeth four times, blow my nose four times, and go to the toilet, putting the lid down and lifting it up four times, then washing my hands four times. I go back to the dormitory counting my steps in fours, pull back the bedcovers four times, take out my contact lenses and put them back in four times, get in and out of bed four times, hang up my dressing gown four times, draw the curtains four times, take off my slippers and put them back on four times, get in and out of bed again four times, say four different prayers four times, touch each corner of the pillow four times, and turn over in bed four times.

Compulsive hoarders

Compulsive hoarding is the intensive collection and retention of large numbers of articles that are useless or of limited value. In extreme forms the compulsive hoarding results in an accumulation of piles of objects that occupy a steadily increasing amount of living space, with the affected person and family members having to navigate their way through mounds of clutter. When a room becomes virtually unusable, it is closed off and the space is turned into an overflow storage area. For example, one patient who engaged in compulsive hoarding filled her double garage to the roof with an enormous collection of articles, none of which she felt able to discard or even sort, and as a result the family vehicles had to be parked on the road. Another patient, who lived in a single bedroom apartment, built up a collection of articles (mainly gifts that she might wish to donate) that gradually occupied the entire bedroom, forcing her to sleep on the couch in the sitting room. Even in this remaining space, she had to thread her way through steadily rising mounds of objects. These objects were placed on the floor and all the furniture, including the bed, with the single exception of one chair which she used for sitting in when she ate or watched television.

In these extreme cases the compulsive need to collect and retain unnecessary objects is first an embarrassment and inconvenience, but then evolves into a source of distress and an inability to function normally. Common collections include business correspondence (receipts, letters, bank statements, credit card receipts), newspapers, household goods from toothpaste tubes to dozens of blankets, timetables, and so on.

Of course, most people will build up a collection of some sort or another, and indeed many people find it difficult to discard some items even when they are no longer in use; however, the intensity, irrationality, and extent of compulsive hoarding is so obviously out of control as to be unmistakable. The distress arises from the unfavourable social consequences of hoarding, plus an anxiety about protecting one's collection, and taking great care to ensure that no one touches or removes or discards items from the hoard. It can impair ordinary functioning because of the severe restrictions it places on the person's daily life, the expense involved, and the inability to allow visitors into one's home.

Compulsive hoarding is often part of a broader obsessive–compulsive disorder, and shares some characteristics of other forms of compulsive behaviour, such as repeated checking. There are differences, however, and these have led to a continuing discussion about whether or not compulsive hoarding is merely another feature of obsessive–compulsive disorder or whether it should be seen as a separate problem. One of the main differences between compulsive hoarding and other kinds of compulsive behaviour is that the hoarding is seldom accompanied by internal resistance that is so typical of most forms of compulsive behaviour. In the clearly obsessive–compulsive problems, the affected person almost always goes through a period during which he or she attempts to fight back and prevent the needlessly repetitive behaviour, such as cleaning or checking over and over again. In cases of compulsive hoarding, however, the person generally feels that the collection and retention of these objects is desirable and even necessary, but simply has got out of hand.

It is important to note that compulsive hoarding is also encountered in a range of other psychological and psychiatric problems and is not associated exclusively with obsessive–compulsive disorder. It is also associated with obsessive–compulsive personality disorder described on p. 32. In addition, a number of people with mental disorders such as schizophrenia engage in compulsive hoarding behaviour. It is also encountered in certain kinds of eating disorders, or among people who have developed psychiatric problems as a result of brain injuries. Hoarding accompanied by self-neglect and living in squalor is considered a characteristic symptom of the condition named the Diogenes syndrome, found in some older individuals. At present there are no reliable figures about the frequency with which compulsive hoarding occurs in these various psychological or psychiatric conditions.

It has been pointed out that indecisiveness is strongly associated with compulsive hoarding, and both appear to be driven by a strong tendency to avoid making mistakes. Compulsive hoarders, for example, will explain their ever-growing collections by a need to ensure that they have the object or item should the need ever arise; they have an inflated fear of the consequences of falling short at some unforeseen time in the future. The indecisiveness is also connected to the great difficulty they have in discarding items from their collection. They experience inordinate difficulty in deciding which items can be discarded and which items it is necessary to retain. Characteristically, when they attempt to sort and discard unnecessary items, they quickly drift into creating new, if smaller, mounds of objects; they engage in what Randy Frost, an American psychologist who has made extensive studies of this problem, has called *churning* of the objects, without actually discarding any of them. Part of the difficulty involved in discarding objects is that many of these people have an inflated fear of the emotional reactions that they might experience if they throw out an item. They fear that they might suffer from a sense of loss. This is particularly true of those items that are hoarded for sentimental reasons, either because of their symbolic value or because of the memories they evoke. In those instances where the person derives an emotional sense of comfort and safety from the collection, fear of loss is readily understandable. Incidentally, in these cases, they attach particular importance to having the collection in view. Some hoarders describe the comfort they feel when they are with their collected possessions. Some, a minority, describe a sense of safety. They need to see the collection or items from the collection. The common belief that compulsive hoarding is the direct result of a period of deprivation, especially in childhood, has not been confirmed by scientific research.

Here is a case example:

A 55-year-old divorced man was referred for help for his compulsive hoarding. The referral was made as a result of complaints by his neighbours (he lived in a block of flats) who feared the risk of fire. He was reluctant to admit that there was a problem, but came for help as he had little choice. When a psychologist and a nurse visited his home with him, they found it almost impossible to get in. The hallway was cluttered with stacks of paper, mostly old newspapers. All the rooms had hoards of items—old, out-of-date food cans, magazines, pieces of cloth, and lots of odds and ends. Most of the furniture was invisible, and the flat smelt of dust and staleness. There was some sort of 'path' to the bed and to the bathroom. The kitchen was too cluttered for any of the appliances to be accessible. In fact the patient had not used the kitchen for a long time; he had to go out for his meals.

The patient's explanation as to why he kept everything was that he was afraid of throwing away 'important papers,' and 'things that might be needed'. It was not clear how he could find anything important or needed in the vast hoards he had.

Those with obsessions unaccompanied by overt compulsions

There is a sizeable proportion of patients whose obsessive–compulsive disorder is characterized chiefly by mental events, with no overt rituals. Some of these have distressing obsessions only, which intrude into their thinking, such as 'My husband may get cancer', 'I am a worthless person', 'God does not exist', 'Am I going mad?', 'Did I say something obscene?', and so on. As noted earlier, obsessions can be thoughts, images, impulses, or—often—combinations of these (see Table 3, p. 15). They occur repetitively and make the patient anxious and uncomfortable.

In some patients, these obsessions are followed by covert compulsions, or mental rituals, which are comparable with overt behavioural rituals in that they result from a strong compulsive urge and usually have the effect of bringing about some relief. Such mental compulsive rituals include silent counting, uttering prayers or certain words and phrases silently, conjuring up certain visual images, and so on. There are some patients who have mental compulsions that are not preceded by any clearly identifiable obsession but, often, patients use mental compulsion as a means of cancelling or neutralizing a preceding obsession or the harm associated with it.

In some patients, the main problem is ruminations. We noted in Chapter 1 that rumination may be seen as a kind of compulsive behaviour, occurring in response to an obsession. The patient engages in long, unproductive thinking about a topic, either of personal relevance or of a religious or philosophical nature.

Case histories

Here is an example of someone with obsessions only.

A young married woman referred herself for help with what she described as 'unwanted ideas' which were about the possibility of her going mad. She had an aunt who had been mentally ill and who spent most of her life in a large mental hospital. For some time, our patient had been assailed by the obsessions 'Am I going mad?', 'Will I end up insane?', 'Will I be locked up?', and so on. Sometimes, she also experienced visual images of herself in a locked-up hospital cell. The thoughts, and the images to a lesser extent, made her extremely anxious and sometimes quite depressed. She reported that the thoughts came 'at least a hundred times a day'. Her husband, to whom she turned for reassurance, somehow did not understand how distressed she was by these, and tended to laugh them off, which made her feel even more helpless. She had no compulsive rituals, either overt or covert.

The following is an example of obsessions with associated mental compulsive behaviour.

A man in his early thirties had the recurrent thoughts that his mother was going to die, although she was in good health. He found it very difficult to dismiss the idea from his mind, and was very upset by this. He developed the compulsive ritual of silently saying 'God is kind, he won't take her away'. He had to say it three times, uninterrupted, which relieved his discomfort. This mental ritual had the effect of 'undoing' or neutralizing the original unwanted thought.

This is an example of a mental compulsive behaviour, with no associated obsession.

A young man had the unwanted compulsion of silently repeating everything other people said in conversation. This meant that he had to be very alert, as he could not afford to miss a single word. The effect of this was that often he could not keep up with conversations, as his own contributions were necessarily limited. At the time he came for help, the compulsion had also spread to what he heard on the radio and television; he often missed the general meaning of what was being said, as he was busy mechanically repeating the words that were being uttered.

Here is an example of ruminations.

A young man had ruminations on the subject of whether he had any heredi-
tary abnormality. The episodes, which were quite frequent, usually began
with the thought 'Am I genetically flawed?' which came to his mind
intrusively. When this intrusion came, he would start his ruminative thinking,
carefully but unproductively trying to think the matter through. This would
include thoughts about his parents, grandparents, and other relatives,
the evidence for their sanity or otherwise, ideas about the heritability of
mental illness, what kind of tests could be done to find an answer to this
question, and so on. The thinking was quite time-consuming and rather
muddled. It never yielded any solution. He would in the end give up, angry
or exhausted.

Mental rituals—a patient's account

The following is an account of an elaborate mental compulsive ritual, as
described by a patient. The man, in his late thirties, reported having had
this problem for over a year. He also had some other obsessive–compulsive
problems, but these were relatively minor ones.

The thought is that something awful is going to happen, not to me but to
my family. It happens dozens of times a day—on some days, over fifty times.
It can happen at any time, but more when I am on my own. Sometimes it is
an accident, sometimes a certain illness, sometimes even death; it is not always
clear which. What is clear is that something terrible is going to happen.
It comes into my mind sharply, all of a sudden, and when it comes I cannot
get rid of it. Whatever I might be doing at the time (say, reading a book) has
to stop. The thought dominates everything else. It makes me quite anxious,
and very tense. I know that it is irrational to worry about my family simply
because of a silly thought but, when the thought comes, I do worry. I then
have to somehow put it right: I have to cancel out the thought. I don't
remember how it began, but what I do now when I get this thought is to
imagine certain things. It is a very fixed sequence. I have to visualize pictures
of my children, my wife, my parents—who are both dead now—then pictures
of the Virgin Mary and Jesus Christ, and then pictures of two other people
whom I happen to know. They have to come in that order, and always the
picture of my daughter Jean has to be imagined before the picture of my
son Tom. When I imagine pictures of the Virgin Mary and Jesus Christ,
they have to have little gold-yellow lights around them. I don't always get

these images easily; in fact, it is often quite a struggle. If it goes wrong or if I am disturbed when I am visualizing these pictures, I have to start again. Most of all, even when I have imagined the whole sequence completely, if I then see something dirty like shoes or a waste bin straight afterwards, then this makes the whole thing worthless, so I have to start again. When it is done without any such mishap, I feel greatly relieved. The tension and the uneasiness all go, and I can get back to whatever I was doing. I somehow feel that I have ensured that the family will be safe, that the disaster that I feared will now not happen. Of course, this is not rational or logical, but that is how I feel at the time.

Getting 'a clear run'

Patients who suffer from persistently intrusive, repugnant thoughts some-times find that actions that are carried out when their nasty thoughts (or images) are present have to be repeated again and again. In order to gain relief they find that they have first to achieve a neutral thought or image, and then carry out the action. For example, a 17-year-old student who repeatedly brushed her hair, taking up to two hours on occasions, explained that in order to feel 'satisfied' with her hair she had to brush it when she had a neutral or good thought in mind. If she experienced one of her objectionable, obscene, intrusive thoughts while brushing her hair, the entire action was spoilt and she had to begin again. On bad days, when the thoughts were especially persistent, she ended up spending long and frustrating periods trying to 'get her hair right'.

Those with primary obsessional slowness

There is a small number of patients, mostly male, whose problem is best described as 'primary obsessional slowness'. This condition was first iden-tified about thirty years ago, and a number of cases have been reported from several countries. Most obsessive–compulsive patients are slow as a result of their ritualistic repetitive behaviour, but in this group, slowness is the *primary* problem; it is not secondary to any rituals. The patient may take half an hour to brush his teeth, an hour to shave, four hours to bathe, and so on. The behaviour is extremely meticulous and precise. Each task has to be done in the self-prescribed correct manner, in the correct sequence, and in an unchanging manner from day to day. The actions most affected in this way are self-care behaviour and other simple tasks of daily living, although, in a minority, behaviour at work is also affected.

In practice, such extreme slowness in self-care behaviour makes a working life virtually impossible.

In one severe case of primary obsessional slowness, the patient took up to six hours to wash and dress himself before starting the day. He felt that he had to shave each separate hair on his face and that his shoelaces had to be exactly equal in length and to be tied with a double knot in exactly the same way each day. His everyday cleaning and dressing was divided into numerous tiny compartments, and each one had to be completed correctly and in the same stereotyped fashion each day.

In primary obsessional slowness, the person rarely resists carrying out the actions in his compulsive, meticulous way. The disorder tends to develop in early adulthood and take a chronic course, leading to increasing degrees of incapacitation. The patients tend to be socially isolated.

Some general comments

Presence of more than one problem

It was noted earlier that most obsessive–compulsive patients have more than one type of problem. Washing and checking often coexist, as do other rituals and obsessions. When describing a patient as a 'washer', a 'checker', and so on, what is meant is that the patient's predominant problem at the time is of such a nature. Furthermore, a patient with one major problem at the time of referral may well have had a different major problem, or problems, in the past. Even within the same problem, the details can change with time.

The significance of numbers

We noted that many patients engage in compulsive behaviour a specific number of times. This is particularly the case with checkers and those with various other repeating compulsions, although many washers and cleaners have special numbers, too. In a good proportion of cases, the special number has some 'magical' significance. The use of numbers also helps patients to remember how far they have reached. Although some patients can explain why a particular number has become significant—for example, the number of one's brothers and sisters, one's birth order, one's husband's birthday—others cannot. Moreover, the key number can change with time.

Avoidance as the main problem

In some cases, the main feature may be not any active compulsive action, but avoidance of something, such as a certain number or a certain colour.

In an earlier section we referred to a young woman who avoided the number four in every possible way (see p. 19)—she did not have any active compulsive rituals, either overt or mental. Some patients avoid washing, checking, or changing their clothes since the activity in question involves exhausting rituals and take up a great deal of time. Some patients with severe contamination fears try to avoid coming into contact with others, leading a reclusive-like life, feeling safe only in their homes, in some cases only in their bedrooms. Howard Hughes, mentioned earlier (p. 36), had an existence marked by such extensive avoidance in the later years of his life.

Indecisiveness

A feature seen in many obsessive–compulsive patients is indecisiveness. This is particularly so for checkers, whose obsessions often appear in the form of doubts, for hoarders, and many of those with other kinds of rituals. However, it applies less often to washers and cleaners. Having to make a decision often triggers off doubting obsessions and related checking and other compulsive behaviour in these patients. In severe cases the difficulty in making decisions effectively renders the patient inactive—the difficulty applies not just to major decisions, but also to very trivial day-to-day matters. For example, one young female patient found getting dressed in the morning almost impossible because she could not decide what clothes to wear. She would put on, and then take off, several dresses. Eventually, her mother had to decide each night what the woman should wear the next day and all her clothes except these were locked away at night. Another patient had virtually given up shopping for groceries because she had such agonizing difficulty in deciding which articles to purchase. It could take her up to fifteen minutes to decide which cereal to select, and extra time to select the particular box of cereal.

Perfectionism

In a proportion of obsessive–compulsive patients, striving for perfection is a feature of their difficulties. They feel very unhappy unless something is done 'perfectly'; and as a result, they often find they repeat things incessantly (e.g. writing a letter), and often do not manage to finish a job at all. One female patient, who was doing postgraduate work at a university, came for help because she was not making any progress with her doctoral thesis. Every sentence was 'imperfect', and she could not proceed with the work until she got a 'perfect' sentence, a 'perfect' paragraph, and so on. She had been 'writing' this thesis for years, yet there was little she could show as a tangible product. Her supervisors were sympathetic, but baffled by her difficulty.

Scrupulosity

Some people with obsessive–compulsive disorder are exceedingly scrupulous. They feel compelled to tell the truth, and do so repeatedly and in great detail, even when no one expresses any interest in their tales. They behave as if they have a hand on the Bible at all times. Their overwhelming need to be totally truthful can be accompanied by attempts to be scrupulously honest. One patient felt compelled repeatedly to tell her relations about her few and trivial amorous indiscretions despite their disinterest, and when their patience came to an end, she tried telling her friends and ultimately her colleagues. A salesman of electronic goods had to be transferred out of sales into the storage department of his company because he insistently gave the customers a full description of all the possible weaknesses, faults, and drawbacks of the products he was supposed to sell. Scrupulosity is related to an inflated sense of responsibility, and in these two illustrations both of the patients were burdened by inappropriately wide and inflated feelings of responsibility.

4
Effect on family, work, and social life

How the family is affected

Quite often, obsessive–compulsive disorder has a significant effect on the other members of the patient's family. This may happen in a number of ways. In some cases, the patient may consistently turn to a family member for reassurance, asking questions such as 'Did I do it right?', 'Do you think I am going mad?', 'Are you sure I did it?', and so on. In most cases, the relatives provide reassurance despite the tiresome nature of the repeated questions. In some cases, family members are requested to carry out some compulsive rituals on the patient's behalf. In others, the patient may demand that others in the family follow certain rules of behaviour, and get very angry if they do not comply. The use of the bathroom is a common source of disagreement and annoyance.

Some obsessive–compulsive patients dominate and rule their families in a remarkable manner. A cleaner with an obsession about dirt may prohibit family members from entering the house with their shoes on, insist on everyone washing their hands and clothes at a certain frequency, totally bar them from certain parts of the house, and impose all sorts of other restrictions. In one case, the patient allowed only a very narrow path through the main lounge, next to the wall, for family members to walk on and—to make matters worse—they had to do this without touching or brushing against the wall! They also had to keep their towels in polythene bags to avoid them coming into contact with the patient's own towels. One young mother did not let her children or husband use the bathroom or kitchen in the morning until she had properly cleaned and washed these places, which took a good deal of time. As a result of this, on many days the husband was late going to work and the children were late for school. Another woman did not cook for her family on most days, since she had failed to clean the kitchen and the utensils satisfactorily in time; so they had to eat out or order take-away meals. A young divorced woman got married for the second time, but would not let her new husband into her house, in case he brought contamination from outside into the house.

Children of obsessive–compulsive patients, especially of female patients, are often made to undergo all sorts of restrictions. They may have cleaning and washing rituals imposed on them, or have to do everything according to a fixed routine. Friends may not be allowed to visit them. When they return from school or play, they may be made to remove their outer clothes and put them into laundry bags before entering house. One woman insisted on bathing each of her children every morning, and this was done in a rigid, ritualistic manner; each child was bathed in turn, washing certain parts of the body first, other parts next, and so on, then dried with a certain number of towels. Another young mother did not allow her son to go anywhere near her husband when he returned from work, until he had a shower and wore fresh clothes. This eventually led to a major marital conflict and the couple separated.

Why do spouses, cohabitees, parents, children, and other relatives tolerate their lives being disrupted and controlled to such a degree by a patient? Many, in fact, respond to the patient's requests and demands initially with questioning or refusal, but in the end give up and begin to comply for the sake of peace. Some family members say that they comply with the wishes of the patient out of love and kindness ('She cannot help it, poor soul'). However, many relatives refuse to comply with the patient, despite quarrels and tantrums. In some families one key member may comply while another is totally unyielding. A teenage girl always received reassurance from her mother about all sorts of doubts and worries she had, but the father never gave her any kind of reassurance. Her mother also complied with numerous demands, keeping the kitchen door open in a certain way, the clock kept facing a particular direction, windows kept open at a certain angle, and so on. The father, however, always refused to comply. This led to the girl's problems causing major conflict within the family.

A mother's account

The following account, given by the mother of a 17-year-old girl with severe obsessive–compulsive problems, highlights the way in which a patient with this disorder can drastically affect the family.

Jenny would get very upset if her things were touched by any of us—even accidentally … Her towel is kept well away from the other towels in the bathroom, her soap is kept separate, and her toilet paper is kept in a paper bag, separate. She insists on the bathroom being thoroughly cleaned by one of us before she goes in, and she spends hours in the bathroom, washing and washing.

Jenny's chair at the dining table is kept covered with a sheet and her plate, mug, and cutlery are kept separate in a drawer. She will eat with us, but not if Ken (her brother) is there. She gets worse when Ken is at home. She says it is not really him but his girlfriend Carol that upsets her. She thinks that this girl somehow makes things dirty, including Ken, and that the whole house is affected. She wouldn't let Ken touch her things at all. Carol is not allowed to come into the house now. Anything sent by her is taboo. She didn't even open the Christmas present that Ken gave her, as she felt that it would somehow make her dirty, as Ken had been to see Carol that day. Now Ken stays away much of the time, and doesn't bring Carol here any more. Poor girl, she is not dirty at all. We all like her, but Jenny won't let us invite her or welcome her. Carol understands and so does Ken, but he still gets very angry sometimes. Some days ago he threatened to bring Carol home for the day. Jenny made such a scene; she said she would leave home for good. In the end, we all felt that Carol should not come … But it is not only Carol and things to do with her. That is the worst, but Jenny thinks most things are dirty. She hardly leaves her room now. Most things in the house she won't go near … She gets me to wash her clothes separately from the others and to dry them separately. You can't reason with her. She gets very upset, or very angry. Once, she made me wash the seats of the car because I had given lift to someone. We are all sorry for her, but we just don't know what to do.

Effects on work and social life

The occupational and social effects of an obsessive–compulsive disorder depend on the severity of the problem. In mild to moderate cases, patients are usually able to continue working and maintain a reasonable social life. However, in severe cases the social and occupational effects of the disorder can be incapacitating.

Many patients manage to continue working by successfully concealing their problems. Slowness and checking, and related doubting, are most likely to affect an obsessive–compulsive person's occupational effectiveness. Their efficiency may gradually become noticeably impaired. A patient with primary obsessional slowness, who required many hours to get ready in the morning, found it increasingly hard to arrive for work on time. He tried to deal with this by waking up earlier and earlier, but eventually he could not keep his job.

Among people who labour under an inflated sense of responsibility, there is a strong tendency to resist any increases in responsibility at work, even to the extent of repeatedly refusing promotion.

Those with washing and cleaning problems may try to find an office room or desk close to the washroom. Their frequent visits to the washroom, or their habit of wiping their desk clean with a wet wipe each morning, may be noticed by colleagues. One young woman kept changing jobs every few months. She eventually confessed to a therapist the reason for her job changes. The moment she was convinced that office colleagues had noticed her frequent hand-washing and cleaning rituals, she would look for new employment. As she was quite an efficient employee, she had no difficulty in getting jobs.

Students with severe obsessive–compulsive problems sometimes have difficulties in their studies. Ruminations may take up a lot of time, as in the case described on pp. 22–23. Repeated checking can sometimes make progress with assignments, or even reading, quite a struggle. As noted above (p. 49), a postgraduate student made no progress with the writing of her thesis because of severe perfectionism. One male student who feared contamination from others gradually stopped going to class, or even to the university library.

If someone spends a great deal of time checking or cleaning, or engaging in other rituals, he has correspondingly less time, or indeed inclination, to engage in social activities. If the disorder is severe, many will become restricted in their social lives. Avoidance of certain places and certain behaviour (e.g., hand-shaking) out of fear of contamination, can understandably lead to a reduction in social contact. Severe fear of contamination can also lead to visitors not being invited or allowed into one's house since they may bring in germs or dirt.

Sex and marriage

We have already described how one's family can be affected by this disorder. It can place an enormous strain on married life. The divorce and separation rates are high for people affected by this disorder, among the highest of any group with psychological or psychiatric problems. It is known that many compulsive hoarders live alone, either never having married or having had a divorce or separation.

If the obsessional fear of concern centres on contamination from bodily products, it is not uncommon to find associated sexual problems. For example, a wife may demand a state of extreme cleanliness before sexual relations, and may insist on elaborate washing and cleaning after intercourse. In some, sex may be restricted to one room or part of a room, to prevent contamination by seminal fluid. In some cases such concerns can lead to a total inability to engage in sexual activity. One married man insisted on his wife taking a thorough bath before he would let her join him in bed. He would sometimes send her back into the bathroom saying that he did not think she had washed herself well enough. Not surprisingly, this led to serious marital disharmony, and they sought help from a marital clinic. It was only during marital therapy that the man's severe contamination fears came to light. He was then referred for help with his obsessive–compulsive disorder. In another case, a man felt that he should have sexual contact only on certain days of the month, linked to the significance he attached to some numbers. He would often invent excuses to avoid intimate contact on other days. It was after more than two years of marriage, and much unhappiness, that he told his wife the truth.

However, in the majority of cases obsessive–compulsive disorder does not necessarily impede the patient's sex life.

5
Prevalence and related factors

How common is obsessive–compulsive disorder?

Obsessive–compulsive disorder is relatively rare, but not as rare as it was once thought to be. Studies have shown that, among psychiatric out-patients, less than 1 per cent suffer from this disorder. Among in-patients the figure is higher, but certainly under 5 per cent. There are, however, problems with figures such as these, since diagnostic practices are not consistent across clinics and hospitals.

The occurrence of the disorder in the general population, rather than among the limited number attending clinics or hospitals, was, until recently, estimated to be about 0.05 per cent—i.e. one out of every two thousand. More recent findings from a systematic survey in selected catchment areas in the United States suggest a much higher figure. A lifetime prevalence of 3 per cent was found in Baltimore. In other words, three out of every hundred persons interviewed had the disorder at some point in their life. The figure was 2.6 per cent in New Haven, Connecticut, and 1.9 per cent in St. Louis. This study also investigated the six-month prevalence rate—that is, how many had the disorder in the six months prior to being interviewed by the researchers. The figures were: 2.4 per cent in Baltimore, 1.4 per cent in New Haven, and 1.3 per cent in St. Louis. A similar investigation carried out in Edmonton, Canada, showed a lifetime prevalence of 3 per cent and a six-month prevalence of 1.6 per cent. A cross-national collaborative study completed in the 1990s, using similar methods in six countries, estimated that the lifetime prevalence was 2 per cent. Many authorities argue that these figures err on the side of overestimation but, even allowing for this, these data show that obsessive–compulsive disorder is more common in the general population than had been suspected.

It must also be remembered that many persons have obsessions and/or compulsions that do not cause sufficient distress or interference with their lives to warrant regarding them as cases of obsessive–compulsive disorder. Even among those whose problems do amount to a clinical disorder, there is undoubtedly a proportion who never seek help; in fact, some positively conceal their problems.

Sex and age

There is no clear preponderance of either males or females among adult patients with obsessive–compulsive disorder. In child obsessive–compulsive disorder, the prevalence is higher for boys (see Chapter 9). There are, however, sex differences in some of the clinical groups within the disorder, which have already been mentioned.

The onset of obsessive–compulsive disorder is usually in adolescence or early adulthood; most cases emerge before the age of 25. In 92 per cent of the cases in one large series of patients seen in a London hospital, the disorder began between the ages of 10 and 40. The onset tends to be earlier in males than in females. It is rare for someone to develop the disorder for the first time after the age of 45. By the age of 30, nearly three-quarters of all identified cases have been diagnosed. A considerable time may elapse before the affected person comes to a clinic or hospital, although prolonged delays are becoming less common. The problem is more readily recognized than it was two or three decades ago.

Marriage, family, social class, and education

Many studies show that a high proportion of adult obsessive–compulsive patients are not married and that there is a greater tendency for male patients to be single than female patients. These patients tend to get married at a later age than most, including other psychiatric patients. There is also evidence that these patients have fewer children.

It used to be widely believed by clinicians that obsessive–compulsive disorder is more common among those in higher social classes and with a higher educational background. This is probably still the case if we look at those who come to hospitals and clinics and are diagnosed as suffering from this disorder, but whether there is a true difference in terms of these social factors is more doubtful. The American catchment area study referred to above did not show a higher prevalence of the disorder among college graduates compared with others.

Course of the disorder

In roughly half of all cases, the problems begin and develop gradually. Among those with an acute onset, there is a preponderance of washers and cleaners over checkers. Generally, the course of the disorder shows some fluctuation. There may be periods when the problem is clearly present and active, followed by relatively good periods. These relatively good periods are, however, not fully symptom-free in most cases. In some, perhaps about half, there is steady worsening of the disorder. We have already noted that the problems get worse with depression. Also, when the person is under stress, the chances of obsessions and compulsions re-appearing, or getting worse, are increased.

Factors that contribute to obsessive–compulsive disorder

It is difficult to give a definitive account of the factors that contribute to the origins of the disorder since the information available is too limited. Data from patients are mostly retrospective, and can be insufficiently accurate.

Precipitating events and stress

Even in cases where a specific time of onset can be traced, a single clear precipitating event is not always found. However, among those where there is a single event preceding the disorder, the onset can be sudden and dramatic—onset within a matter of days or even hours of the precipitating event is not unknown. In one case, a man developed severe obsessive–compulsive problems related to fear of illness immediately after undergoing surgery for the removal of a non-malignant growth. In another, a young woman who was brutally sexually assaulted while on holiday abroad found herself thoroughly and repeatedly cleaning herself and throwing away the things she had with her at the time, almost immediately afterwards. This rapidly developed into full-blown contamination fears and extensive washing and cleaning rituals. In an earlier chapter (see pp. 29–30) we noted that a small proportion of patients who develop post-traumatic stress disorder after a catastrophic experience may also develop clinically significant obsessive–compulsive problems.

Cases of clear and dramatic onset linked to a severely traumatic personal experience are not very common. On the other hand, stressful experiences of various sorts in the period of time preceding a more gradual onset of the disorder are frequently reported. These include overwork, pregnancy and childbirth, problems in marriage or sex life, illness, and death or illness of a close relative. In a significant minority of cases, the onset of obsessive–compulsive disorder is preceded by an episode of depression.

There are no known links between the nature of onset and outcome, or between the type of precipitating event and outcome.

Pollution of mind

Many victims of sexual assault report feelings of intense dirtiness but it is not merely dirtiness of the usual kind. They experience what can be described as a strong sensation of internal dirtiness that has emotional overtones. 'Things look clean but they feel dirty, shameful. Even after I have taken a shower my friends can tell that I am dirty. It is gross. I feel sullied.' This form of internal dirtiness, usually referred to as a sense of mental pollution, can arise even without physical contact with a dirty object or situation. It is also associated with a number of disturbing emotions, among which feelings of shame, disgust, and embarrassment are prominent. Unlike other forms of dirtiness, mental pollution is not responsive to washing or cleaning. A patient described how she would take five, six, or seven showers in rapid succession in her vain attempts to eliminate the sense of internal dirtiness. Frequent showering had so damaged the wooden floor in her bathroom that it had to be entirely replaced. When asked why one shower was not sufficient, she explained that at best it would give her some marginal relief and as she was left with a strong sense of dirtiness she felt compelled to repeat the shower, over and over again. This unresponsiveness to ordinary washing is a characteristic of feelings of mental pollution. These feelings can be induced by physical contact which the person finds disgusting, or even by information, and can also be revived by memories in the absence of any physical contacts. Given these qualities, it is not surprising that feelings of mental pollution tend to be so persistent. In order to overcome obsessive–compulsive disorder in patients with a dominant sense of mental pollution it is necessary to deal with this component of the disorder.

Parental influence

Are there parental influences? If a child grows up in a household where one of the parents is severely affected by obsessive–compulsive disorder, is it likely that he will also develop the same problem? Many children briefly display comparable behaviour, but very few ever develop obsessive–compulsive disorder. Children of an affected parent seldom develop lasting, specific compulsive behaviour. If anything, they are more likely to develop over-dependence and timidity.

Heredity

What about genetic factors—is the disorder inherited? The kinds of studies that are needed to conclusively answer this question do not exist. Of the available twin studies, comparing the occurrence of the disorder in pairs of identical (monozygotic) twins with the occurrence in non-identical (dizygotic) twins, some appear to suggest a higher rate of concordance (that is, both twins in a pair having the disorder) for identical pairs, while others have reported different findings. The same applies to studies of family members. A study carried out in London, which compared the first-degree relatives (father, mother, brother, sister, son, daughter) of fifty obsessive–compulsive patients with those of a matched group who did not have the disorder, showed that the former group had a higher rate of lifetime psychiatric problems—that is, the relatives of the obsessive–compulsive patients had more psychiatric disorders in general at some time in their life, than did the relatives of the control group. However, no greater incidence of obsessive–compulsive disorder itself was found among this group.

Taken together, the available studies suggest that there is a genetic contribution, but that this does not make someone vulnerable to obsessive–compulsive disorder specifically. What appears to be inherited is a general emotional oversensitivity which can predispose one to the development of some form of anxiety disorder.

Culture and obsessive–compulsive disorder

Obsessive–compulsive disorder is found in different parts of the world, and in different cultural settings. Descriptions are available for most Western cultures, as well as India, Pakistan, Hong Kong, Japan, Taiwan, Egypt, Singapore, and Sri Lanka, among others. The similarities of the obsessions and compulsions found in diverse countries are remarkable; the features reported in a large series of obsessive–compulsive patients in India were not very different from those found in studies in the United Kingdom or the United States. A very early Buddhist text has an interesting account of a monk at the time of Buddha (over twenty-five centuries ago), who engaged in what can only be described as compulsive behaviour. It is reported that the monk, called Sammunjani, spent most of his time sweeping the monastery with a broom and that this activity took priority over everything else. The Japanese Zen master Hakuin (1685–1768), a major figure in the history of Zen Buddhism, is described as having suffered from severe obsessive–compulsive problems as a young man. The main feature of this appears to have been obsessional thoughts in the form of doubts.

This period in the life of Hakuin, who was a major religious leader in the Far East, bears interesting comparison with one stage of the life of an even more influential religious leader in the West, Martin Luther. Luther (1483–1543) is reported to have been tormented by recurrent and severe doubts and intrusive, blasphemous thoughts. At this time he had, for example, doubting thoughts that he might have carried out all sorts of acts that were sinful. He also had recurrent doubts as to whether he had confessed fully and properly.

Similar unwanted intrusive thoughts of a blasphemous nature also affected John Bunyan (1628–88), the author of *Pilgrim's Progress*. He gave a vivid account of these in his autobiographical book *Grace Abounding to the Chief of Sinners*, which was first published in 1666. One of his great fears was that, instead of words of praise for God, he might utter terrible and blasphemous thoughts. He had to resist this with great effort, and was very distressed by these unwanted thoughts. In a particularly informative passage, Bunyan describes one of his unwanted thoughts in these words:

> But it was neither my dislike of the thought, nor yet any desire and endeavour to resist it, that at the least did shake or abate the continuation of force and strength thereof; for it did always in almost whatever I thought, intermix itself with, in such sort that I could neither eat my food, stoop for a pin, chop a stick, or cast mine eye to look on this or that, but still the temptation would come, *Sell Christ for this, or Sell Christ for that; Sell Him, Sell Him.*

The phenomena of obsessions and compulsions are not confined to one culture or one period of time. The basic features are essentially the same across diverse cultural backgrounds and eras. However, some of the specific contents of the obsessions can reflect common concerns found in a particular culture or era. For example, obsessions and compulsions related to fears of contamination by asbestos was a relatively common problem among patients with obsessive–compulsive disorder in Britain twenty to thirty years ago. More common in recent years have been obsessions, and associated compulsions, with the theme of HIV/AIDS.

Another way in which culture has some influence on the nature of obsessive–compulsive disorder is religion. The content of a patient's obsessions can reflect religious beliefs and ideas. Studies in India have shown a preponderance of obsessive–compulsive disorder with themes of dirt and contamination among Hindu patients; this is seen as reflecting the preoccupation with matters of purity and cleanliness in that culture. A study from Israel, looking at obsessive–compulsive symptoms in a sample of thirty-four patients, found symptoms linked to religious practices in thirteen out of nineteen ultra-orthodox Jewish patients, but in only one out of fifteen non-ultra-orthodox Jewish patients. Further, those with strong religious beliefs appear to be prone to developing clinical obsessions as a result of attaching high significance to unwanted intrusive thoughts. Blasphemous or sexual thoughts, for example, may cause a lot of distress in those brought up in a strict religious background. This distress can then lead to the perpetuation of the thought, turning it into a clinically significant obsession.

Obsessions and compulsions across the age spectrum

The elderly

While the onset of obsessive–compulsive disorder is uncommon in elderly people, there are exceptions. A small number of people may develop the disorder at a late age. Also some, with an earlier onset, continue to suffer from obsessive–compulsive disorder into old age. Recent reports show that some elderly patients have obsessional thoughts that reflect concerns related to their stage in life.

One patient, in his early seventies, had the recurrent thought: 'What will happen to me when Phyllis dies.' Phyllis was, of course, his wife, and she was eight years younger. The patient knew that the chances of her dying before him were not high, and he was fully aware that his thoughts were irrational. He also had a vivid, terrifying visual image of his wife dying, which often accompanied the thought. He reported that the thought came to him over a hundred times a day. He was very distressed by this and sought help.

Other cases of elderly patients with similar obsessions have also been reported.

The relatively small literature on this subject shows two other recurrent themes in obsessive–compulsive problems in old age. One relates to aspects of physical functioning, the other to religious and moral concerns.

Children and adolescents

Obsessive–compulsive disorder can occur in childhood and adolescence, and there is a growing literature on this subject. A discussion of childhood obsessive–compulsive disorder is provided in Chapter 9.

6
Theories and explanations

Different theories have been put forward in attempts to explain obsessive–compulsive disorder. It is not possible, in a short book like this, to attempt a full discussion of these theories. What we shall do in this chapter, instead, is to take a brief look at some of them.

The psychoanalytical view

Historically, the oldest and best-known theoretical account is the psychoanalytical one. Psychoanalysis is the treatment technique for neurotic disorders that was developed by Sigmund Freud, and the assumptions underlying it are referred to as a 'psychoanalytical theory'.

In this view, obsessions and compulsions are seen as symptoms of some deeper problem in the person's unconscious mind. Certain memories, desires, and conflicts are kept out of consciousness, or repressed, because they would otherwise cause anxiety. These repressed elements may later manifest themselves as neurotic symptoms. Fixation (or 'getting stuck') at a particular stage of development, caused by various factors during one's formative years, determines the nature of the neurotic symptoms that appear in this way in later life. Obsessive–compulsive disorder is linked in this way to the stage of development that is called, in this theory, the 'anal–sadistic stage', in which toilet training is a major feature. Anger and aggression are also associated with this stage of the child's development. Certain experiences during this phase, including desires, impulses, conflicts, and frustration, can make one vulnerable to obsessive–compulsive disorder, and to obsessive–compulsive personality features, in later years. The compulsive acts, obsessional thoughts, and so on are seen as defensive reactions that suppress the real, hidden anxieties.

There are many versions of the psychoanalytical theory of obsessive–compulsive disorder, including some recent contributions. Some of them have led to interesting and extensive theoretical discussion. However, there is little evidence to support the psychoanalytical theory, in its various forms. It is also one of those theories that cannot easily be tested.

There is no satisfactory evidence that psychoanalytical treatment is effective for obsessive–compulsive disorder.

The learning view

The other classical psychological theory that attempts to explain obsessive–compulsive disorder is the learning view. This is also referred to as the behavioural view. This considers that neurotic disorders, and many other behavioural problems, are predominantly acquired or learned. An individual may learn, through association with a painful or terrifying experience, to become anxious about certain things that are really harmless. He may also learn that certain behaviour reduces anxiety, and this then becomes strengthened. In this case, the compulsive behaviour, because it reduces anxiety, becomes established and strengthened; the person thus engages in this behaviour as a habitual way of reducing or preventing anxiety.

There is evidence that, in most cases, the carrying out of the compulsive behaviour indeed reduces anxiety or discomfort. The discomfort coming from one's own obsessions, or from various events and objects around one, is generally reduced by the performance of the rituals. So, the compulsive behaviour is maintained because it is an effective way of reducing discomfort.

Another piece of evidence that gives some support to the learning view comes from animal studies. In certain experimental settings, animals placed in aversive or painful situations are seen to engage in previously learned anxiety-reducing behaviour in a stereotyped, repetitive way, even though this behaviour does not lead to any relief or escape from the current situation. This suggests that, in stressful situations, previously useful anxiety-reducing behaviour may be rigidly resorted to, even though it has no logical relationship to the present stress. The seemingly senseless ritualistic behaviour of some obsessive–compulsive patients may be seen as a similar phenomenon.

However, the learning view has difficulty in providing a comprehensive explanation of these problems. As we noted earlier (p. 59), many patients with obsessive–compulsive disorder do not recall any initial painful experience or experiences as the starting point of their problems; that is, there is often no clear direct learning experience. Also, the theory gives no explanation as to why only certain kinds of things—e.g. dirt, germs, and so on—and not others, commonly become the subject of concern and lead to obsessions and compulsions. It also fails to explain the origin of the obsessions themselves, particularly those that are senseless—e.g. order, patterns, symmetry, and so on—and those, though meaningful, that have no relevance to the person's history or present life.

The cognitive behavioural view

A theoretical account that adds a cognitive component to the learning—that is, behavioural—view has been developed in recent years. This approach takes into account the person's cognitions—beliefs, thoughts, etc.—as an important aspect of the problem. It is noted that many patients have an exaggerated appraisal of risk and danger. Many also have an exaggerated sense of being personally responsible for avoiding/preventing harm and disaster. The way one appraises one's own cognitions is also seen as contributing to the development of some form of the disorder. There are signs that this new, expanded account will lead to better understanding and improved results. Already two detailed and specific cognitive theories have been developed, one to account for obsessions and the other for checking.

Biological causation

Within the past few decades, it has been suggested by several authors that obsessive–compulsive disorder is caused by a biological disturbance. The biological theory proposes that the disorder is caused by a biochemical imbalance in the brain—in particular, it has been claimed that obsessive–compulsive disorder arises because of an inadequate supply of serotonin. (Serotonin is a neurotransmitter—i.e. a chemical substance that carries messages between cells in the brain. It is known that serotonin plays an important part in brain functioning.) This theory originally emerged from the finding that an antidepressive drug, clomipramine, which blocks the natural loss of serotonin, can produce therapeutic effects in these patients.

The biological theory has gained some support, but has also been criticized. Therapeutic effects of equal or greater magnitude than those produced by clomipramine or similar drugs have been achieved through purely psychological treatment methods—when the serotonin level is ignored. There is no evidence that people suffering from obsessive–compulsive disorder have serotonin levels that differ from those of people suffering from other comparable psychological disorders, especially other anxiety disorders, or levels that differ from people free of any such disorder. Furthermore, there is no relationship between the amount of clomipramine absorbed and the degree of therapeutic change. Even with high doses of the drug, and hence high levels of serotonin, relatively few patients are free of obsessive–compulsive symptoms and some patients simply do not improve. It has also been found that the patient's initial response to clomipramine does not provide a good basis for predicting the longer-term effects of this medication. Additionally, on present evidence, the most effective anti-obsessive drug is clomipramine, which is even more effective than comparable drugs that are superior boosters of serotonin levels.

Another criticism of the biological theory is that the attempt to decide the cause of a disorder from a therapeutic effect is risky. For example, the fact that aspirin relieves a headache tells us little about the cause of the headache, and it certainly does not tell us that the headache occurred because the person was short of aspirin. The fact that clomipramine often reduces obsessive–compulsive symptoms does not mean that the disorder was caused by a shortage of clomipramine, or of the serotonin that it bolsters.

A great deal of research is being carried out at present on this issue. No doubt, in the next decade or so, a good deal of new light will be shed on the biological theory by these studies. The evidence supporting the theory is not persuasive at the moment.

Other approaches

Some writers have offered the view that obsessive–compulsive patients' problems are the result of a cognitive defect—i.e. a deficit in their thinking, or thinking style. The well-known difficulty of many obsessive–compulsive patients in making decisions is often cited as evidence of this. There are also some experimental results that show certain thinking patterns in most of these patients. However, the available evidence is far too weak to give support to the view that a cognitive defect or a particular cognitive style is the explanation of this disorder. Much more and far stronger evidence is needed before this can be properly evaluated, let alone accepted, as a valid explanation.

Conclusions

There is, then, no satisfactory theory at present that can give a comprehensive account for obsessive–compulsive disorder. It is possible that different aspects of the problem need different explanations. Of the currently available theories, the cognitive behavioural one, which incorporates the old learning view, has the most supporting evidence, but further developments are awaited. It appears, from the available data, that many factors are involved in the genesis and persistence of this disorder. As noted previously, genetic and family factors may make it more likely that someone develops these problems. It is also clear that stressful experiences have some part, probably a very important one, to play. There is substantial evidence that stressful emotional experiences can lead to recurrent intrusive thoughts and images in people. It has been suggested that when a traumatic or stressful experience is not fully emotionally processed—i.e. resolved or absorbed—it may leave residual effects that manifest themselves as various symptoms. In this way, recurrent intrusions that are normally short-lived may become chronic and persistent in some people. Perhaps this is how some obsessions get established in the first place. Some recent clinical reports that document the development of the disorder following a seriously traumatic experience in some people (see pp. 29–30) provides some support for this. We believe that this is a plausible account, although it needs to be properly tested before it is accepted as a valid explanation.

However, the lack of an accepted explanation does not mean that we are in a helpless position with regard to the treatment of this disorder. As with many other problems, the development of effective treatment techniques for obsessive–compulsive disorder has far outpaced the development of explanations for why and how it occurs in certain people.

7
Treatment

Many obsessive–compulsive patients can now be successfully treated, in contrast with the situation even as recently as the 1960s, when there was almost a resigned acceptance that little could be done to help them.

Cognitive behaviour therapy

This change has been brought about mainly by the development of behaviour therapy, later expanded into cognitive behaviour therapy. Obsessive–compulsive disorder is now considered to be a good candidate for treatment using this approach, with encouraging results.

What is cognitive behaviour therapy?

Cognitive behaviour therapy grew out of behaviour therapy. Behaviour therapy, also called 'behaviour modification' and 'behavioural psychotherapy', refers to the use of learning theory in the treatment of psychological disorders. Learning theory is the body of knowledge and ideas that psychologists have developed on the basis of hundreds of studies of how changes take place in human and animal behaviour. Use of this knowledge, and techniques based on it, for human behavioural problems was always considered possible, and several people in the early part of this century reported such use. However, it was only in the 1950s that it developed into a formalized treatment approach. This was largely because of the work of the South African psychiatrist Joseph Wolpe (1915–97), who later practised in Temple University, Philadelphia. The work of Hans Eysenck (1916–97) in London contributed greatly to the development and acceptance of behaviour therapy as a major approach to certain psychological problems, which views many behavioural problems as learned. They are seen as cases of faulty—or maladaptive—learning, or as cases of failure to learn.

In either case, it should be possible to correct matters by applying the principles of learning: the faulty learning can be undone, and new learning can be promoted. Therefore, behaviour therapy concentrated on the problem of behaviour itself. It did not assume, as the psychoanalytical approach did, that the difficulty is a symptom of deeper unconscious problem. Rather than attempting to unravel an assumed root cause, behaviour therapists worked directly on the problem behaviour. They concentrated more on the problem as it is now, and what factors are currently associated with it, rather than its past history. Of course, therapists need to know from the patient when the problem started, how it developed and so on, but the main focus is on the problem as it is now and the therapist's efforts are geared towards modifying this problem.

The efficacy of behaviour therapy for a range of psychological disorders is well established. For many of these, it is now considered by many practising clinicians as the treatment of choice. The early criticism that if a problem is treated directly by behaviour therapy, without going into its 'unconscious roots', it will later lead to other symptoms, has been shown to be unfounded—there is no evidence that such symptom substitution takes place.

In recent years, the scope of behaviour therapy has been expanded to include aspects of what is known as 'cognitive therapy'. Cognitions are thoughts, ideas, beliefs, and attitudes. Cognitive therapists focus their treatment on elicitation of the patient's cognitions that are relevant to his problems and on helping him to modify them. The most impressive work by cognitive therapists so far has been in the treatment of depression and panic. Depressed patients often have very negative thoughts such as 'I am a worthless person', 'There is no point to my life', and so on. Attempts are made to modify these thoughts using a variety of techniques, including challenging them, assembling evidence to the contrary, and setting up behavioural tasks where they are disconfirmed. The use of cognitive therapy was first established in depression, and these principles and techniques are now being used for other disorders as well, notably panic disorder (see the book *Panic disorder* in this series—full reference in Appendix 8). Many incorporate these principles within a behaviour therapy framework, and the term 'cognitive behaviour therapy' is now used to characterize this approach.

In the case of obsessive–compulsive disorder, there is a clear role for cognitive therapy techniques—including steps to prepare the ground for the implementation of behaviour therapy, and to help prevent a return of the problem once treatment is over. The patient's beliefs about risk, danger, responsibility, and so on often play a part in obsessive–compulsive disorder, and eliciting and helping to modify these can be a key aspect of treatment. A clear example of value of the cognitive therapy in this way can be seen in the treatment of a typical compulsive checker. Most such patients have an excessive sense of responsibility. The patient believes that he is responsible for the safety and well-being of a whole range of people; hence the excessive, repetitive checking of gas taps, electrical switches, and so on. The identification of this exaggerated sense of responsibility and a consideration of its irrationality and untoward consequences can be a most useful step in treatment. Promising results have also been reported in the cognitive treatment of obsessions. It is said that the obsessions persist because the person attaches great personal significance to the unwanted, intrusive thoughts (e.g. 'Having these thoughts means I am a sinful/dangerous person'). The therapeutic reduction of such false appraisals can lead to great relief and improvement. This kind of cognitive work plays an important part in therapy for obsessive–compulsive patients.

Cognitive behaviour therapy is in the process of further development and one can reasonably anticipate important advances in the near future.

Exposure and response prevention for those with overt rituals

The systematic application of behaviour therapy to obsessive–compulsive disorder goes back to the mid-1960s when a psychologist in London, Victor Meyer, began to treat patients who had compulsive rituals with what he called 'apotrepic therapy'. It consisted of two elements; placing the patient in real-life situations that made him feel anxiety or discomfort and triggered off his compulsive urges (*in vivo* exposure); and preventing the patient from carrying out his compulsive behaviour (response prevention). This combination of *in vivo*—or real life—exposure plus response prevention soon became very well established as a technique for treating patients with overt compulsive behaviour. Research in Britain, the United States, and The Netherlands further developed and refined this treatment and provided convincing evidence of its efficacy. It remains the treatment of choice for these patients today.

It should be noted that some authors and clinicians refer to the therapy as 'flooding and response prevention', because the exposure carried out in this treatment is usually intense and prolonged, hence the word 'flooding'. This will become clear in later sections, when the details of such therapy are described. In this book, we shall use the more descriptive term 'exposure'.

Rationale

Before describing the details of this form of treatment, we need briefly to note the rationale behind it. Typically, an obsessive–compulsive patient with overt behavioural compulsions experiences discomfort and a strong urge to ritualize when provoked by the occurrence of the obsession, or by exposure to the trigger stimulus or situation. When the patient engages in the compulsive behaviour (say, hand-washing) the level of discomfort goes down. But what would happen if the discomfort and the urge to engage in the compulsive behaviour were provoked, but the patient was then prevented from carrying out the compulsion? Several studies have shown that, in this situation, the level of discomfort and the strength of compulsive urges still go down, but much more slowly. When this is done in repeated sessions, day after day, there is a cumulative effect, leading to the patient feeling progressively lower levels of discomfort and weaker urges to engage in the compulsive behaviour. Also, the urges and discomfort decline progressively more quickly as treatment progresses.

The role of modelling

In the practice of therapy, modelling is often added as a third element in the treatment package. This refers to the therapist carrying out the action that he instructs the patient to do—touching door handles, for example—in the presence of the patient, by way of demonstration. He does this in a calm and controlled way, with no sign of anxiety or discomfort. He also models coping with this exposure, without needing to wash and clean. Modelling facilitates therapy, and often is needed to encourage a fearful patient to carry out certain behaviour needed in treatment. It is, however, not an essential ingredient. The essentials are exposure and response prevention.

Imaginal exposure

In some cases, imaginal exposure, also called 'exposure in fantasy', is used. This may be done for situations that it is not practical to expose the patient to in real life, and also as an initial step to prepare the patient for *in vivo* exposure to a situation. Some research in the United States suggests that, for patients who fear that disasters may occur in the future if they do not engage in their compulsions, imaginal exposure to these disasters may be a useful additional element in therapy. A patient may be asked, for example, to imagine, very vividly and clearly, a bloody accident or air crash involving a loved one—the disaster he fears. Such imaginal exposure is claimed to improve the long-term results of therapy, when used in addition to *in vivo* exposure and response prevention, but its value remains to be confirmed.

Therapy in practice

How is the treatment done? It is important to stress that different therapists will set about their task in different ways, although the same principles are involved. So, the account given below should not be taken as a definitive account of what all therapists do, but rather as an example that highlights the general principles and issues.

In the assessment (see below) the therapist obtains detailed information from the patient about the full range of his difficulties. At this stage, the patient's beliefs and attitudes relevant to the problem are explored and discussed. The rationale for the treatment is also discussed in detail. The therapist and the patient then discuss the priorities and decide which compulsion, or set of compulsions, will be treated first. For each selected target, the therapist asks the patient for a full account of the objects or situations that trigger the obsession and/or lead to his compulsive rituals. A list is constructed, indicating how difficult these triggers or cues are for the patient to face. This is usually done by asking the patient to give a rating of discomfort that he estimates he will experience in each of these situations, usually on a scale of 0–100 (where 0 means 'no anxiety or discomfort' and 100 means 'extremely severe anxiety or discomfort'). An example of such a list, or hierarchy, is given in Table 4. Similar ratings may also be obtained for the strength of the compulsive urge, with 0 indicating 'no urge' and 100 indicating 'extremely high, irresistible urge'.

Table 4 An example of a hierarchy of problem situations of an obsessive–compulsive patient

Items	Discomfort rating (0–100)	Compulsive urge[a] rating (0–100)
Using a public toilet	100	100
Touching the inside of the kitchen waste bin	95	90
Touching the toilet seat at home	80	85
Touching the outside of the kitchen waste bin	70	75
Picking up something from the kitchen floor	70	70
Shaking hands with a stranger	65	55
Using a public telephone	60	50
Touching door handles in a public place	55	45
Bumping into a stranger	55	50
Touching money given by a cashier in a supermarket	50	35

[a] *The strength of the urge to engage in strenuous hand-washing after the activity concerned.*

The therapist and the patient then agree on where in this list, or hierarchy, exposure should begin. Ideally, it is best to tackle a high point, even the highest, early on, but in practice, many patients are reluctant to agree to this. The starting point is often the highest item that the patient is willing to try despite his discomfort, provided it is not too low in terms of discomfort and compulsive urge. He is then exposed to this in an active, even exaggerated, way. Exposure to several related items may be tackled together. For example, if the concern is with dirt and germs on the floor, door handles, and so on, the patient is asked to touch very thoroughly, with the therapist usually first modelling the actions, several door handles, the floor, the rim of the dustbin, and so on. The 'contamination' may then be spread to his arms and clothes by getting him to rub his hands on them. This exposure is followed by a period of response prevention. The patient refrains from washing or engaging in any other cleaning ritual. The therapist usually stays with him during this time. It is extremely rare for a patient to need to be actually physically restrained from engaging in the compulsive behaviour. In fact, most therapists agree that this should never be done, since the patient needs to be sufficiently motivated to comply with the response prevention instructions—if this is not the case, no amount of coercive work will be useful.

The therapist will be sympathetic about the patient's discomfort, and will help to make it easier for him—e.g. by distraction, conversation, and so on. The response prevention period with the therapist may last for two hours or so; by this time, the patient's discomfort arising from the exposure, and the related compulsive urge, will normally have come down considerably. If they are still high, the session will be continued until there is a significant reduction, particularly in discomfort. The patient is instructed not to engage in the ritual even after this time period. Normal washing is allowed, as needed for reasons of hygiene, but the patient must not ritualize or exceed the set limit. After normal washing, the patient may be instructed to recontaminate himself so that the exposure continues. In some programmes there is strict round-the-clock supervision, but with the majority of patients this is not usually necessary.

Another important requirement in this therapy is not to give reassurance. The patient may ask for reassurance from the therapist or, at home, from a family member. These requests are not complied with. Family members are instructed not to give any reassurance. If, for example, the patient asks 'Are you sure nothing will happen?' or 'Are you sure it is all right?', the family is asked to respond with something like 'We agreed not to talk about that, didn't we?' or 'Remember, your therapist told me not to answer such questions'.

It sometimes happens that a patient, out of his great unease during the response prevention period, engages in brief, unnoticeable rituals, or even mental rituals as a temporary substitute for the real ones. These possibilities are usually discussed by the therapist with the patient before the programme begins, so the patient will do his best not to resort to such means, which can only frustrate the therapy. Equally, in the exposure part of the treatment, a patient may touch the contaminating object very briefly and/or just with the tips of his fingers or the back of his hand. This does not help, as the resultant discomfort and the compulsive urge may then not be very high. Again, the therapist usually explains that proper exposure is needed, and makes sure that this happens.

It is possible to expose the patient continuously, for hours or even days, to the discomfort-arousing stimuli. For example, if animal fur is the major source of discomfort, the patient may be asked to carry a small packet of dog hair in his pocket all the time. A patient with obsessions about the colour black may be instructed to wear black underwear and to sleep on a pillow that has a black pillowcase.

Sessions are held quite frequently in the early stages of treatment. Numerous stimuli or situations are used from the hierarchy, or from several hierarchies. The patient is told at the outset about the need for a good deal of time to be set apart for therapy. Because of the time factor, a therapist may also use others as co-therapists, or helping therapists, who need to be fully familiar with the patient's problems and the details of the treatment programme.

It is preferable for the patient not to be taking anxiolytic drugs at the time of treatment. Those who have been taking medication such as diazepam (e.g. Valium) may be taken off it, or have the dosage reduced, because the anti-anxiety effects of the drug may impede the effects of exposure and response prevention treatment. As mentioned above, the rationale for this type of approach is that the anxiety or discomfort must be provoked, and then extinguished by allowing it to dissipate spontaneously. So any drug, including alcohol, that blocks or reduces the anxiety may hinder this effort.

The details of the programme always depend on the individual patient's problems and how the therapist plans to deal with them after joint discussion—no two patients are alike, and the therapist has to develop a suitable programme for each case. When the therapy is done on an out-patient basis, which happens in the vast majority of cases, a family member may be enlisted as a co-therapist who can help with supervision, or even extra sessions, at home. Patients are given specific homework sessions to supplement the work in the clinic. If an in-patient programme is used, either because of the severity of the problems or practical difficulties in implementing therapy on an out-patient basis, attempts will be made to carry out most of the sessions away from hospital and in the home situation as soon as it is practicable. A family member may be invited to participate in some of the therapy, even in hospital.

A case illustration—the treatment of a compulsive washer

Here is a case example illustrating the exposure and response prevention therapy package.

A 22-year-old male undergraduate was referred with extensive washing rituals, related to obsessions he had about being contaminated by dogs. Specifically, he feared that he might catch rabies (although he knew that the chances of this were slim) or some other serious infection. He engaged in repeated and time-consuming washing rituals every time he felt he was contaminated; this would happen if he passed a dog or saw a dog faeces on the road, if someone who had been with a dog came near him, or if he happened to touch or brush against anything to do with dogs, like a discarded collar or a lead, or a feeding bowl. He also had a great deal of avoidance behaviour. He would cross the road to avoid having to pass a dog. He began to avoid friends and others whom he knew had dogs (in the end, he stopped going to classes). He would throw away any item of clothing he happened to be wearing when he went past or got anywhere near a dog. His life became very restricted as a result of this. He had no other obsessive–compulsive behaviour except some minor checking rituals which were not causing any problems.

Initial cognitive exploration showed that the patient recognized the irrationality of his behaviour, but he did not feel confident about this. The rationale of the behavioural treatment was explained to him, which he was able to accept. He was treated with exposure and response prevention, with modelling. A list of situations which caused him anxiety was prepared on the basis of ratings of severity given by him, on a 0–100 scale. He was willing to accept exposure to the highest four items in this list. These were: touching a dog with both hands (anxiety 100); touching a bowl from which a dog had eaten (anxiety 90); touching a piece of cloth which had come in contact with a dog (anxiety 80); and walking barefoot on the ground where dogs had previously been (anxiety 75). The exposure to the first three items involved him having to touch the item very thoroughly, and then rubbing his hands on his clothes and arms. He had agreed not to wash his hands or take a bath, nor to change the affected clothes, for a period of three hours after each session. He had three or four treatment session a day. He had to keep with him, all the time, a piece of cloth which had been rubbed thoroughly on a dog in his presence, even keeping this under his pillow when he slept to ensure continuous exposure.

Despite being anxious to begin with, he cooperated well with the programme and, within a few days, was very much improved. The lower items in the original list (e.g. holding the hand of someone feeding a dog, anxiety 50) did not prove too difficult when he was later asked to do them. He began to display fewer and fewer avoidance behaviours, and began to move freely and use public transport.

This patient maintained his gains well. At one stage, several months later, when he noticed some signs of the problem returning, he treated himself, as he now knew what the principles of therapy were, and quickly brought the problem under control.

Therapy for other overt rituals

Although the example above was about the treatment of washing and cleaning compulsions, the principles of exposure and response prevention are applicable to all compulsive rituals. For checking compulsions, the patient is asked to engage in behaviour that provokes checking (e.g. leaving the house, closing drawers, putting things into envelopes and sealing them, switching off electrical appliances, and so on), and then to desist from carrying out the checking. An effort is made to ensure that no reassurance is given. In the treatment of checking, the primary components are reducing the inflated responsibility and preventing the checking compulsions. The former is dealt with using cognitive techniques.

Those with compulsions to do certain things in certain bizarre ways are asked to engage in this behaviour in other, more normal, ways. For example, a patient who does not leave a room without touching the four walls will be taken into and persuaded to leave rooms, but with no touching. Someone who has to have his table and wardrobe arranged in a very rigid way, will be made to disarrange the things on the table and in the wardrobe, and discouraged from putting them back in his compulsive fashion. In short, any overt compulsions can be treated by this approach.

Reduction of avoidance

All these programmes need to have built into them the reduction of avoidance behaviour. Even after successful therapy focused on difficult target situations, a patient may still avoid many other situations, partly out of habit and partly because of residual worries. Patients are therefore encouraged to go out of their way to expose themselves to all sorts of situations that can provoke rituals, not just those to which they have been exposed in the therapy sessions.

In cases where the major problem is compulsive avoidance, the main therapeutic strategy is to expose the patient extensively to the avoided situations or things. Let us illustrate this with two case examples.

The first is a young woman who avoided the number four, described on p. 19. You will recall that she did this in her obsessional belief that, if she did not, her husband would come to some harm. This avoidance behaviour extended to all areas of her life and dramatically restricted her functioning. The treatment given to her included exposing her to the number four in numerous ways, many of them continuous. She was persuaded to do many activities four times, she had the number four painted on the walls and ceilings of her room, she carried pieces of paper with the number four written on them in her pockets and handbag, and so on. She achieved considerable improvement very quickly.

The second example is the woman who had obsessions about cancer, described on pp. 18–19. She had extensive avoidance behaviour at the time of referral and was admitted to hospital. She avoided anything she feared might lead her to discover signs of cancer. Her treatment programme consisted of getting her to engage in all the behaviour that she avoided, initially with supervision and help. For example, she was regularly made to look at herself in a full-length mirror, to wash and bathe herself, to make her bed in the morning, to wash her underwear without looking away, to palpate her breasts, and so on. She had long sessions with the nurse during which she carried out these activities, very thoroughly. This treatment programme led to considerable improvement within a short period of time. At five years' follow-up, she was still free of the problem, and leading a normal life.

Results of therapy

If the therapy is carried out properly and consistently, the results of cognitive behaviour therapy, including exposure and response prevention, can be quite impressive. There may be initial distress, and some patients may even want to give up therapy, but, once this stage has passed, it becomes easier. The therapist needs to be supportive but firm, and to have a good relationship with the patient. A substantial amount of therapy time may be needed: dozens of sessions rather than two or three, and each session needs to be long, at least initially. When the patient repeatedly experiences reductions in discomfort and in his compulsive urges despite being exposed to whatever he is worried about, his own confidence increases. The new freedom he begins to feel as his problem gradually comes under control is very rewarding. One patient said 'I can go anywhere now. I can do so many things which I couldn't even imagine myself doing. This is wonderful.'

This freedom, paradoxically, can be a problem. If the patient has been severely affected for some time, he may have had a very limited life, socially and otherwise. The family, too, is likely to have developed a lifestyle revolving around the patient's problems and demands. The patient's improvement now gives both him and his family a good deal of freedom and free time. New activities, or restarting of old activities, are needed. In short, they have to readjust to normal life. Most therapists nowadays will make it a point to help patients and relatives by counselling them in these matters.

Treatment of obsessions

The progress made around thirty years ago in treating compulsive behaviour, notably compulsive cleaning and compulsive checking, was not accompanied by comparable advances in dealing with obsessions. However, recently some progress has been accomplished, mainly by changes in our understanding of the nature of these unwanted, repugnant intrusive thoughts. As noted earlier it seems likely that these intrusive thoughts, which are experienced by almost everyone at one time or another, can become transformed into obsessions if and when the person interprets them to be of great personal significance. The thoughts are interpreted by the person as being revealing, and as signifying that he is immoral, evil, dangerous, insane, or a combination of these qualities. These patients may also believe that the thoughts will lead to catastrophic consequences and fear that they might lose control. The thoughts are extremely distressing, and can give rise to attempts to put matters right, to neutralize, conceal, or suppress the thoughts, and also to avoid places or people that might trigger the thoughts.

As a result of this new analysis of obsessions, the primary aim of treatment has shifted away from the earlier methods and now focuses on the patient's interpretation of the thoughts. The therapist aims to assist the patient in making more realistic and accurate interpretations of the significance of the unwanted, intrusive thoughts. This involves an analysis of the thoughts and the meaning that the patient places on them.

The earlier methods of treatment included thought-stopping, distraction, repeated exposure to the intrusive thought (by encouraging the patient repeatedly to form the thoughts to instruction), re-shaping the intrusive images by deliberate exercise, and by discouraging the avoidance of situations in which the person was inclined to re-experience the intrusive thought. These methods continue to have their uses, but are no longer the core treatment. For over thirty years, thought-stopping was used by therapists in an attempt to help the patient achieve control over the unwanted and usually uncontrollable thoughts. The therapist asks the patient to relax and close his eyes. The patient is then asked to verbalize the obsession or thought, and when he does, the therapist shouts 'Stop!' loudly. The procedure is repeated several times and in the second stage, the patient is asked simply to form the thought, and to indicate to the therapist with a pre-arranged signal when he has accomplished the formation. At this point the therapist interrupts the thought by shouting 'Stop'. This too is repeated several times. In the next stage, the patient himself shouts the word 'Stop' and after some training will move on to the final stage where he makes the stop command silently to himself. There are also variants of thought-stopping, which include thought-switching or thought-substitution, and they all share the same purpose of helping the patient acquire the ability to dismiss the unwanted thought and think another thought, usually a pre-selected pleasant one, in its place. Another variant uses a mildly aversive stimulus—a rubber band worn on the wrist, which the patient pulls and releases against the wrist at the same time he gives himself the silent stop command. Thought-stopping can be helpful but is seldom sufficient and nowadays plays a subsidiary part in treatment at most.

Another approach is to get the patient deliberately to form the thought to instruction, and in some ways this is the opposite of thought-stopping. It is sometimes referred to as 'habituation training', in which the aim is to get the patient to become accustomed to the unwanted thought. As a result of repeated and/or prolonged exposure, the thought gradually becomes less and less upsetting, and eventually should no longer arouse anxiety or discomfort. In this application the patient is asked to get the thought and keep it focused in his attention, dwelling on it without losing it. In this way he can be exposed to the thought for up to an hour at a time. In practice, most people are unable to retain a specific thought for longer than a few minutes at time. During treatment they are asked repeatedly to re-form the thought to ensure prolonged exposure. An alternative way of ensuring prolonged exposure is to ask the patient to write out the thought repeatedly. Another variant is to ask the person to make a tape recording of a description of the obsession and then to listen to the audiotape repeatedly. An advantage of this method is that the exposure can be continued at the patient's wish and is not confined to sessions at the clinic.

In all types of treatment, whether the early methods or new variants, an essential component is to encourage the person to avoid avoiding—that is, to reduce and hopefully eliminate all avoidance behaviour that is designed to keep the person away from situations in which he might experience the obsessions. This kind of strong and persistent avoidance behaviour may be temporarily successful but ultimately fails to control the anxiety, and it is best eliminated. Avoidance behaviour may even reinforce the obsessions.

As there is a close association between obsessions and depression, the presence or emergence of depression can lead to an increase in the intensity or frequency of the obsessions, and in these cases treatment of the depression, if necessary by antidepressant medication, should be considered.

The main shift in emphasis that has been taking place during the past few years can be described as a movement away from helping the patient to cope with the unwanted and uncontrollable thoughts to actively undermining their occurrence by helping him to substitute more realistic and accurate interpretations of the significance of the intrusive thoughts themselves. This is essentially a cognitive behavioural approach, with much cognitive input.

The problem of images

In some cases the obsession takes the form of mental imagery (see Table 3, p. 15). When the main problem of the patient is an intrusive image, special techniques have been used. With some practice one can learn to manipulate and 'play about' with one's mental images. In experiments, normal subjects have been shown to be able to rotate, expand, shrink, and otherwise manipulate their visual images. This facility can be improved with practice. If an obsessive–compulsive patient complains of distressing images, he may be instructed to deal with the image by modifying it in various ways. A patient whose unwanted, intrusive image was of dog faeces, was trained to shrink the image smaller and smaller, until it became just an innocuous dot. Another patient who complained of distressing images of a violent scene was trained to focus on a marginal detail of the image and 'zoom in' on this part. In this way it was possible to make this part of the image, which did not arouse discomfort, larger and larger, so that the discomfort-arousing part of the image 'overflowed' from the image space. The image thus became less upsetting. Techniques such as these for manipulating one's unwanted images are probably effective because of the sense of control the patient achieves in successfully manipulating them. After all, one of the reasons why obsessions are a problem is that they intrude despite one's resistance and are hard to dismiss. If, therefore, the patient achieves some control over the image, that makes it less of a problem.

While these image-manipulation techniques are useful, they are not the main treatment for intrusive images. The new cognitive approach used for intrusive thoughts, described above, is equally applicable to images. Like thoughts, the images are distressing because the person attaches undue significance to them, and so helping the person to interpret them in a different way is the core treatment.

Treatment of compulsive hoarding

In cases of compulsive hoarding, treatment is usually difficult because of fears, especially fears that arise from the threat of other people touching, rearranging, or discarding the collection. Until recently, most therapists took the view that the best that could be done was to help hoarders adopt procedures for reducing or limiting their collection in order to make their everyday life more tolerable. This was a steady, gradual process, marked by occasional purges. The patient would be persuaded to let a therapist help with the disposal of agreed items, and when this was the case better and speedier results were achieved.

Here is a case example:

A middle-aged-man (see p. 44) who had severe hoarding problems was treated behaviourally. His cooperation was less than ideal to begin with, but after some persuasion he agreed to cooperate in the programme. He had vast hoards of papers, tins, food cans, pieces of cloth, and numerous other items. Two therapists joined him in inserting quantities of stuff into large refuse bags, which were disposed of. He first insisted that he wanted to check each item before agreeing to dispose of it, but this became so time-consuming that he relented on this after the first day. Parts of the house were cleared in an agreed order. The hallway and the kitchen were the priorities. The patient was pleased that he could now use his kitchen (which had been impossible before), but he still felt that some important, or potentially useful, things were lost.

Following this progress, treatment was focused on how to prevent further hoarding. It also included help with developing contacts and interests outside the house.

Recent reports show that a comprehensive cognitive behavioural treatment approach can be effective. Such a programme would include education/information about hoarding, help with organizational and decision-making skills, re-structuring of cognitions related to hoarding, and actual behavioural work. The behavioural work focuses not only on discarding collected items, but also on refraining from acquiring new items to hoard. This comprehensive approach appears to be a promising development in the treatment of hoarding.

Therapy for primary obsessional slowness

For those patients whose problem is primary obsessional slowness, a therapy involving pacing, prompting, and shaping is used. The patient's behaviour is paced, with repeated urging to speed up. Time limits are set for selected behaviour and the patient is helped to keep to these time targets. The therapist assists by prompting the patient. Some modelling may be used as well: the therapist may demonstrate, for example, how to comb one's hair in just two minutes, and get the patient to do likewise. The patient is also given feedback on how well he is doing, and praised for completing a behaviour quickly. A selected target behaviour may be 'shaped', in the sense that the time allowed for it in each session is gradually shortened.

This kind of treatment is very time-consuming and requires a great deal of input by the therapist. Some of these patients require hospital-based treatment initially, and after the in-patient phase, much home-based therapy is also needed. These patients improve only gradually, and may not retain their improvement unless further help is given by booster sessions. Fortunately, patients in this category are few in number.

A case illustration

An example illustrating the treatment of primary obsessional slowness is given below.

A 38-year-old man with chronic and severe obsessive–compulsive disorder was referred for treatment. The main feature of his disorder was excessive slowness—he took roughly three hours to prepare himself for work each morning. He bathed infrequently because he needed up to five hours to complete the process. By the time he was referred for help, he was in danger of losing his job because he was regularly quite late for work.

In the treatment programme, a wide range of self-care behaviour was dealt with. Only the management of brushing his teeth is cited here, as an example. Initially, he was advised and instructed on how to brush his teeth in a reasonable length of time. This produced a small impact; soon a plateau was reached beyond which no improvement took place—a typical feature with these patients. Then, the patient was asked to carry out the brushing in the presence of the therapist for a few occasions; it was clear that the slowness resulted from his wish to brush each tooth in turn, in a particular sequence, and in a meticulous manner. He was then given a demonstration of brushing teeth at normal speed, and he was asked to imitate the therapist. Some improvement was obtained immediately. In the next stage of therapy, he was instructed to brush his teeth on a number of occasions during which the therapist set up a speeded-up goal and provided time checks every thirty seconds. This produced further improvement, although the patient found it difficult to break the five-minute barrier, which was the agreed goal.

Following this approach in dealing with all of his problems, a significant overall improvement in bathing, washing, teeth-cleaning, and dressing was achieved. He gradually learned to complete his daily self-care chores in an acceptable manner and period. The improvements ensured that he was able to retain his job.

Other behavioural techniques

Various other behavioural treatments have also been used with obsessive–compulsive patients. One is systematic desensitization, in which the patient imagines problem situations in a graded series of steps while under relaxation. This was a common treatment of phobias in the early days of behaviour therapy, and is still used in some cases. Sometimes this also includes real-life exposure to situations. In this procedure, anxiety or discomfort is kept to a minimum, in contrast to the exposure and response-prevention approach, where discomfort is provoked.

Contingency management is an approach that manipulates the consequences of a behaviour. For example, if a patient's rituals receive a lot of positive attention and sympathy, an attempt may be made to ensure that rituals cease to produce favourable results. Instead, alternative behaviour is rewarded. Sometimes, aversive procedures are used; e.g. a mild electric shock, or the use of a rubber or elastic band for obsessions. These techniques have been shown to have only a limited effect.

The use of contingency management does play an important part as an additional element in therapy, in some cases. If it is clear that the patient's obsessive–compulsive behaviour has become very rewarding to him, then the results of any exposure and response prevention programme may be lessened by this factor. For example, a rather shy and timid young man who had severe obsessive–compulsive problems, including excessive avoidance of going out, was treated with standard therapy but the results were short lived. It quickly became clear that the disabilities caused by the problems (inability to go out, to wash his own clothes, to do any outdoor work, and so on) had the effect of his mother doing everything for him and waiting upon him. It was necessary to break this pattern of events through counselling sessions in which the mother was fully involved, before the young man's problems could be brought under control effectively. This is a somewhat atypical example, but the general principle that it illustrates is clear. Do the obsessive–compulsive symptoms bring any 'benefit' (such as attention, endearing words, or work being done for him) for the patient? Therapists will normally look into this in their analysis of the problems. Such an analysis, which looks closely into a problem behaviour and its triggers or antecedents on the one hand, and its consequences on the other, is called 'functional analysis'. If a functional analysis shows that the symptoms do lead to such 'benefit' for the patient, some work will be undertaken to change this pattern, in addition to the main treatment techniques used.

Sometimes, these patients are taught muscle relaxation. This is a fairly simple procedure in which one is instructed to relax all the major muscle groups in the body in a series of exercises. Some early therapists using thought-stopping had the patient in a relaxed state for this procedure, although this was not seen by many as an essential ingredient. Training in relaxation can help obsessive–compulsive patients in an indirect way; stress and tension tend to make one's obsessions and compulsions worse. Sometimes, the problem reappears after a relatively clear period of time, in the wake of stressful experiences. Therefore, if one learns to relax oneself as a means of coping with stress and of reducing tension, it can be of considerable use later.

A simple guide to relaxation is given in Appendix 1.

Problems in therapy

Effects of depression

It is known that the chances of an obsessive–compulsive patient benefiting from cognitive behaviour therapy are reduced if he is very depressed. These patients are best treated after their depression has been relieved by other means, psychological or pharmacological.

Motivation and cooperation

Some patients find the demands of a cognitive behavioural treatment programme prohibitive. They may either refuse to accept the therapy offered, or show poor cooperation and tend to drop out. Therapists usually make an effort to persuade a reluctant patient to accept the treatment offered, by answering their queries in detail and pointing out that the chances of improvement are high. A reluctant or doubting patient may be helped by the opportunity to talk with a successfully treated patient. In the end, however, the patient must decide for himself whether or not to accept therapy. Careful cognitive therapy at the preliminary stages often facilitates treatment acceptance and cooperation. It is important to ensure that the patient is well motivated. A patient with low motivation to change is unlikely to benefit much from treatment. Such a patient is unlikely to adhere fully to the instructions of a treatment programme. In cases where a patient is pressured into therapy by family members, the results tend to be poor unless the patient himself sees the need to comply. A therapist will carefully assess a patient's motivation to accept therapy, before undertaking to treat him.

Other types of psychological treatment

Psychotherapy

By 'psychotherapy' we mean psychoanalysis or other forms of psychodynamic therapies. They share the assumption that the obsessions and/or compulsions of the patient are symptoms of underlying unconscious problems. The aim of the therapy, carried out in sessions in which the patient is encouraged to 'free associate' (to speak openly and at length about feelings and thoughts), is to unravel these hidden factors (the 'real' problem) and resolve them. The relationship that develops between the patient and the therapist is also considered important, and is said to play a part both in bringing to surface deep-rooted conflicts and memories and in resolving them. A patient may be seen twice weekly, or even more frequently, for two or three years. The results of this kind of therapy have not been shown to be satisfactory, particularly for obsessive–compulsive disorder. Sometimes, a patient may report that regular psychotherapy sessions have given him a better understanding of the problem or a better outlook on life, but the specific complaints rarely improve beyond what might happen if the problem was left untreated. This form of therapy is usually available only privately, so it can be expensive.

Hypnotherapy

Claims made by some practitioners for the effectiveness of hypnotherapy, usually involving strong suggestion to the patient while under hypnosis that he will no longer experience obsessions or compulsive urges, are not supported. There is no satisfactory evidence that hypnotherapy has much to contribute in treating these patients. Some patients and/or their families are fascinated by the very idea of hypnotherapy and ask for it when they come for help, but faith in its efficacy is misguided.

Group therapy

Treating patients in a group setting is sometimes undertaken by therapists for various conditions. For example, patients with difficulties in social skills are often treated in social skills groups. There is, as yet, no persuasive evidence that group therapy has any special role to play in the therapy of obsessive–compulsive patients. However, in some recent treatment programmes, patients have been treated successfully in groups. Further, support groups for patients have been found to be of some benefit when used as an adjunct to individual therapy. Family members may also be included in the support groups. In recent years, self-help organizations (see Appendix 7) have been running support groups for patients and families, and many have found these to be helpful.

Systemic therapy

In this approach, a problem or a symptom that a patient has is sometimes viewed as serving a function for the wider system—such as family or husband–wife dyad. To return to the case described on pages 86–87, do the patient's inability to wash his clothes, do any outdoor work, etc., and the resultant overdependence on the mother, serve any function for the mother, or the family? Are they enjoying their overprotective role? It is certainly possible that in some cases this dimension is relevant. Family work focusing on these issues will be beneficial in such instances, in addition to the standard therapy.

Non-psychological treatments

Drug treatments

Many psychiatrists believe that pharmacological treatment is of considerable value in obsessive–compulsive disorder, and there is evidence that some types of medication are effective.

Sometimes, patients are given anxiolytic benzodiazepine drugs such as chlordiazepoxide (e.g. Librium) or diazepam (e.g. Valium). Usually, they give temporary relief from the feelings of anxiety or tension, but tend to have little effect on the obsessions and compulsions themselves. These drugs can also be habit-forming. Phenothiazines such as chlorpromazine (e.g. Largactil) are also occasionally prescribed, but there is seldom real benefit from them.

Antidepressant drugs are often prescribed, and varying degrees of success have been reported. In those many cases in which the obsessive–compulsive disorder is compounded by depression, direct treatment of the depression by drugs or psychological methods is needed. As noted earlier a severely depressed obsessive–compulsive patient is unlikely to benefit from, or indeed effectively engage in, cognitive behavioural treatment. In such cases, the first priority is to treat the depression. In some, the successful treatment of the depression is followed by alleviation of the obsessive–compulsive problems, and additional treatment may not be necessary. In others, reduction of the depression leaves the obsessions and compulsions weakened, but still handicapping and distressing. Additional treatment is then required.

The alleviation of depression that accompanies obsessive–compulsive disorder can be achieved by standard antidepressant medication. A list of these drugs is given in Appendix 2.

Strong claims have been made that the tricyclic antidepressant clomipramine (Anafranil) is of particular value in the treatment of obsessive–compulsive patients. It is possible that it is particularly efficacious in reducing depression in these patients, but whether it also has a specific effect on obsessive–compulsive disorder is still a matter for debate. In a major study carried out in London in the 1970s with the support of the Medical Research Council, it was observed that clomipramine did reduce both depression and obsessive–compulsive problems in a group of patients who suffered from both. However, in those patients who had little depression, clomipramine failed to produce significant improvement. The results of more recent studies do not provide a consistent picture. On balance, the evidence points to the conclusion that clomipramine is an effective treatment, especially when depression is also present; but the improvements are seldom complete, and a significant minority of patients do not benefit from the drug. Recent research also suggests that the initial response to clomipramine does not provide a good prediction of the longer-term effects of this medication. Patients tend to relapse when they stop taking the drug.

Common side-effects of clomipramine include: dryness of the mouth, constipation, dizziness, nausea, drowsiness, weight gain, and impairment of sexual functioning—particularly difficulty reaching orgasm. It can also cause cardiac arrhythmias in overdose, and is not prescribed where there is a risk of overdosing.

Clomipramine is usually started with small doses, gradually increasing to 100–250 mg a day, as necessary. Most patients take between 150 and 200 mg. The response to the medication is not immediate; it can be several weeks before any effect is seen.

Of the other antidepressant drugs tested in recent years, encouraging results have been achieved with fluoxetine (Prozac) and fluvoxamine (Faverin, Luvox). These belong to the group of drugs called selective serotonin re-uptake inhibitors (SSRIs). Other drugs in this group include paroxetine (Seroxat, Paxil), sertraline (Lustral, Zoloft), and citalopram (Cipramil). These, too, have been used in the treatment of obsessive–compulsive disorder.

Table 5 Antidepressants used in the treatment of
obsessive–compulsive disorder

	Starting dose and increment[b]	**Usual target dose**[b]	**Maximum dose**[b]
Clomipramine[a]	10–25	100–250	250
Citalopram	20	40–60	60
Fluoxetine	20	40–60	80
Fluvoxamine	50	200	300
Paroxetine	10–20	50	60
Sertraline	50	150	225

[a]*Clomipramine is a tricyclic; all others are selective serotonin-re-uptake inhibitors.*
[b]*These are adult doses and are given in milligrams.*

These values are based on the recommendations made by a panel of international experts as guidelines for clinical practice. Reference: March, J. S., Frances, A., Carpenter, D. and Kahn, D. A. (1997). Treatment of obsessive-compulsive disorder (Expert Consensus Guideline Series). Journal of Clinical Psychiatry, 58 (Supplement 4).

Reports suggest that SSRIs have fewer side-effects than clomipramine. They are also safer in the event of overdoses. However, they are not free of side-effects. Common side-effects of fluoxetine are nausea, vomiting, some insomnia, and initial increase in anxiety. Fluvoxamine can lead to headache, reduced appetite, and sweating.

The overall, long-term value of these drugs in the treatment of obsessive–compulsive disorder is still to be determined. On current evidence, long-term benefit depends on the continuation of medication. There is a high chance of relapse when the drug is withdrawn.

Antidepressants used in the treatment of obsessive–compulsive disorder and the recommended dosages are given in Table 5.

Some psychiatrists recommend the use of these drugs along with psychological treatment. For those obsessive–compulsive patients who find it difficult to accept a cognitive behavioural treatment programme, initial treatment with suitable medication can help. Additional cognitive behavioural treatment will help to maintain the treatment gains.

Psychosurgery

In the past, many patients with obsessive–compulsive disorder were treated with psychosurgery—that is, surgery on the brain. Psychosurgery was originally introduced as a potential method for treating schizophrenia, and was then extended to other problems, including obsessive–compulsive disorder. The operations are used far less often now than they were few decades ago. In fact, psychosurgery is now seen as a treatment of last resort.

Psychosurgery is an invasive and drastic form of treatment, although the techniques used are now much more refined than they were, and therefore have fewer side-effects, than in the early days. Also, several different surgical procedures are used nowadays (unlike in the early days when the only procedure was leucotomy, which consisted of destroying a small part of the white matter of the brain in the frontal lobes). Although, moderately favourable results have been claimed in some patients with chronic intractable rituals or obsessions, in many others the results of psychosurgery have been unsatisfactory. Moreover, some patients who do report some improvement say that they still have just the same obsessional thoughts and so on, but that they are less troubled by them. There is no evidence that psychosurgery is nearly as effective a form of therapy as the non-invasive psychological techniques.

Electroconvulsive therapy (ECT)

Occasionally, severe obsessive–convulsive patients have been treated with ECT (also called electric shock therapy). In this procedure, convulsions or fits are induced by passing a small electric current through the brain from electrodes applied to the head, while the patient is under the effects of a short-acting anaesthetic and a muscle relaxant. It is painless, and the patient retains no memory of the procedure. There is no evidence that ECT has any beneficial effects on obsessive–compulsive disorder.

8
Diagnosis, assessment, and evaluation

In the section on the practical aspects of cognitive behavioural treatment, we discussed briefly some of the ways in which a therapist assesses obsessive–compulsive problems. Therapists of different orientations and backgrounds will assess these problems in slightly different ways, but some aspects of assessment are almost universal.

Aims of assessment

One aim of assessment is diagnosis, and psychologists, doctors, and psychiatrists will look particularly for diagnostic features when a patient is seen initially. The criteria commonly used in the diagnosis of this disorder are the ones listed in Table 2 (see p. 2). Diagnosis is not usually a problem with obsessive–compulsive patients, although there can be some puzzling cases.

Once the diagnosis is established, further and more detailed assessment is undertaken. The main purpose of this is to gather information for devising a treatment programme. As these patients are usually best treated by a cognitive behavioural approach, detailed information is needed to enable an effective treatment plan to be carried out. Therapists—whether psychologists, psychiatrists, nurse therapists, or other professionals—will therefore enquire in detail about various aspects of the problem. This is also linked to a further aim of assessment—namely, to evaluate the effects of treatment.

How is assessment done?

The main techniques of assessment use by therapists are summarized in the following paragraphs.

Interview with the patient

The main mode of the assessment is the interview. This may take, on average, two or three hours, spread over more than one session. In this, the patient will be asked for full details of the problem(s), including how they affect his work, relationships, and social life. Questions will be asked about how and when it all started and what the course of the disorder has been, including fluctuations in severity, relationship to stressful events, and so on. As for the problems themselves, close enquiry will be made about each presenting problem, and the person's thoughts about all of them.

For obsessions, these enquiries will focus, among others, on the following aspects. What is the content of the obsession? What form (i.e. thought, image, or impulse, or a combination) does it take? Is it triggered by any event or object? How long does it last when it comes? How does the patient try to get rid of it? How much anxiety or discomfort does it lead to? Does it lead to a compulsion? What is the personal significance of the obsession? What does it tell us about you? Is it revealing of anything important to you?

For compulsions, the questions will include the following examples. What events of objects lead to the urge? How strong is the urge? How frequently does it occur? What is the actual nature of the compulsive behaviour? Is it an overt (motor) behaviour or a covert (mental) behaviour? How long does it last? Does it need to be performed a certain number of times? What is the significance of that number? How much does the patient resist the urge? What happens if the compulsive behaviour is interrupted? What does the patient think or believe will happen if he does not carry out the compulsion? Does he feel a special responsibility to prevent such consequences by personally carrying out the ritual?

The therapist will also ask about how much avoidance there is, whether there is any reassurance seeking and, if so, from whom, and whether any other members of the family are involved in the rituals. Normally, all the aspects of obsessive–compulsive phenomena summarized in Table 3 (see p. 15) will be gone into in some detail.

The therapist will also explore the relationship between the problems and mood, and may ask several questions about depression.

In addition to the conventional diagnostic interviews used by most clinicians, a number of specialized methods have been developed for purposes of clinical research and/or in clinics that provide specialist treatment for obsessive–compulsive disorder. These specialized interviews are called 'structured' because the diagnostician follows a carefully constructed, strict manual which ensures that the questions are asked in exactly the same manner and sequence for every patient, by every interviewer. The structured interview schedules used in assessing obsessive–compulsive disorder range from a broad scale which assesses mental health in general (the SCID, Structured Clinical Interview), to a scale that focuses exclusively on anxiety disorders (the ADIS, Anxiety Disorders Interview Schedule), and finally to the most specific scale which provides assessments of the nature and severity of the obsessive–compulsive disorder (the Y–BOCS, Yale–Brown Obsessive–Compulsive Scale). As the scales become more specialized, they enable the clinician (or research worker) to increase the 'magnification of the microscope'.

Self-ratings

Most therapists will ask the patient to rate the discomfort and the urge to ritualize on a numerical scale. Some use a 0–10 scale, others prefer a 0–8 scale, while still others use a 0–100 scale. The last mentioned is easy for the patient to use and is recommended by many. Sometimes, especially with children, a visual analogue scale is used instead. This is simply a straight line, usually 100 mm in length, one end of which indicates the highest possible level of what is being measured (such as extremely high discomfort), and the other the absence of it (e.g. no discomfort at all). The patient indicates where, on this line, his response lies. The therapist can convert this into a numerical score by simply measuring the distance from the 'low' end to the place marked by the patient, as in Fig. 1.

No discomfort _____ Extremely high
    at all   discomfort

Figure 1 A visual analogue scale sometimes used for rating discomfort

In preparation for therapy, various situations (e.g. using a public telephone or leaving the house without checking gas taps) that are relevant to the patient's problems will be listed, with ratings of discomfort and of compulsive urge. For each main problem, a separate list or hierarchy may be prepared. An example of such a list was given in Table 4 (see p. 75).

Interviewing others

Interviewing a family member or other key informant is also part of the assessment, whenever possible. Some aspects of the patient's problems are often more clearly described by a family member than by the patient himself. For example, problems and stresses caused by the patient's behaviour and the demands on the family may be minimized in the patient's own account.

Sometimes a patient has no realistic idea of the extent of his own disability, and information from the family or other informants will be most valuable. Occasionally, information may be sought from work colleagues or employers. Contact with family and employer is made only with the patient's consent.

Behavioural tests and direct observation

Sometimes a therapist may carry out one or more behavioural tests with the patient. For example, a patient with contamination fears about dirt and germs on door handles, public telephones, and so on, may be asked to touch a door handle during the interview session. The patient's reaction, his attempts to avoid this, and his ratings of the discomfort felt while carrying out the action, are all important information for the therapist. Behavioural tests may also be carried out at home or, less frequently, at work. Direct observation at home or at work may also be undertaken. For example, a man whose obsessional slowness began to affect severely his efficiency at work was observed by the therapist for a set period of time, with prior arrangement.

Record-keeping by the patient

It is common for a therapist to ask the patient to keep a daily record of his problem behaviour for a week or two prior to starting therapy, as a baseline measure. It may be continued during therapy as a way of monitoring progress. The record can either be an open-ended account in which the patient writes in detail what happens, or more commonly, a record using a structured format provided by the therapist. An example of a structured record form is given in Fig. 2 and a completed record form in Fig. 3. As can be seen, the record focuses on selected target problems which are briefly recorded. Such structured records are easier to use and much more amenable to analysis than open-ended accounts. Another problem with open-ended accounts is that many obsessive–compulsive patients religiously write pages and pages of detail. One patient who was asked to keep a written record of his daily problems for a week produced a sheaf of over a hundred pages in very small, neat handwriting!

Questionnaires and inventories

Standard questionnaires and similar instruments are also used in assessment. These have the advantage of covering a range of difficulties and producing a numerical summary score. However, these are not used as a substitute for interview, but as an additional measure. Checklists, questionnaires, and inventories are often used in this way. Some patients find it extremely difficult respond to questionnaire items, and spend hours

Date: Target:[1]

Time	Frequency[2]	Highest discomfort[3]	Highest compulsive urge[4]	Details and comments[5]
Before 7 a.m.				
7–10 a.m.				
10 a.m.–1 p.m.				
1–4 p.m.				
4–7 p.m.				
7–10 p.m.				
After 10 p.m.				

1   The particular obsession or compulsion monitored.

2   How many times it happened in each time period.

3, 4   Rated on a 0–100 scale; give the highest felt during the time period.

5   Details of what happened: when, where, what was the trigger, how long taken, number of repetitions, and so on, of the worst episode.

Figure 2 An example of a daily record sheet, blank

agonizing over the precise accuracy of their replies. If the completion of the questionnaires takes excessive time or is upsetting, they can be omitted or delayed.

Some commonly used instruments are described below.

The Maudsley Obsessional–Compulsive Inventory

A widely use self-report instrument for obsessive–compulsive patients is the Maudsley Obsessional–Compulsive Inventory (MOCI), which was developed in the 1970s at the Maudsley Hospital in London. The MOCI consists of thirty items. The patient has to choose either 'true' or 'false' for each item.

Date: 27 September   Target:[1] Hand-washing

Time	Frequency[2]	Highest discomfort[3]	Highest compulsive urge[4]	Details and comments[5]
Before 7 a.m.	2	70	70	After using toilet. Washed hands with soap, 3 mins.
7–10 a.m.	3	80	85	After journey to work by bus. Felt quite dirty. Washed with soap, 4 mins.
10 a.m.– 1 p.m.	0			In office all the time.
1–4 p.m.	2	60	60	After going to the toilet. Washed with soap, 3 mins.
4–7 p.m.	3	85	90	Felt very dirty after return journey in crowded bus. Washed with soap, 5 mins.
7–10 p.m.	1	40	45	Before supper. Washed without soap, 1 min.
After 10 p.m.	2	70	75	After cleaning toilet. Washed with soap, also arms, 5 mins.

1   The particular obsession or compulsion monitored.

2   How many times it happened in each time period.

3, 4 Rated on a 0–100 scale; give the highest felt during the time period.

5   Details of what happened: when, where, what was the trigger, how long taken, number of repetitions, and so on, of the worst episode.

Figure 3 An example of a daily record sheet, completed

The inventory yields an overall obsessive–compulsive symptom score, and, in addition, separate subscores for checking, washing and cleaning, slowness and repetitiveness, and doubting and conscientiousness.

These are a few items from the MOCI:

- I avoid using public telephones because of possible contamination.
- I use only an average amount of soap.
- Some numbers are extremely unlucky.
- I do not tend to check things more than once.
- One of my major problems is that I pay too much attention to detail.

The full inventory and the scoring key are reproduced in Appendix 3 and Appendix 4.

The MOCI is easy to use, and has been shown to be a useful part of assessment. It has been established as a standard instrument in several countries.

The Compulsive Activity Checklist

This instrument is used both for self-rating by the patient, and for ratings by the therapist. The Compulsive Activity Checklist (CAC) lists thirty-nine specific activities (e.g. having a bath or shower, brushing teeth, cleaning the house, switching lights and taps on or off, touching door handles, filling in forms, eating in restaurants, and throwing things away). Each activity is rated on a four-point scale of severity, for 0 (no problems with the activity) to 3 (unable to complete of attempt the activity). The total score is obtained by adding the scores of the individual items. However, the total score is less important than the range of activities that present problems in the patient's life, and the identification of those activities that are impossible or extremely difficult to complete.

The CAC was developed in the 1970s at the Maudsley Hospital in London. It is used regularly in many clinics and hospitals.

The Padua Inventory

The Padua Inventory (PI) was developed by Ezio Sanavio in Italy. It has sixty items, scored from 0 (not at all disturbing) to 4 (very much disturbing). Thus the range of scores is from 0 to 240. The PI has recently been used and standardized in some other countries as well.

Here are some items of the PI:

- I feel my hands are dirty when I touch money.
- I wash my hands more often and longer than necessary.
- Before going to sleep I have to do certain things in a certain order.
- I sometimes have an impulse to hurt defenceless children or animals.
- When I hear about a disaster, I think it is somehow my fault.

The Obsessive–Compulsive Inventory

The Obsessive–Compulsive Inventory (OCI) was developed a few years ago and has already begun to be used widely. The OCI consists of forty-two items. It has seven sub-scales: washing, checking, doubting, ordering, obsessing, hoarding, and mental neutralization. For each item, a rating scale is used for both frequency and distress, over the past month. For frequency, a five-point rating scale used, from 0 (never) to 4 (almost always). For distress, again a five-point rating scale is used, from 0 (not at all) to 4 (extremely).

The Yale–Brown Obsessive–Compulsive Scale

The Yale–Brown Obsessive–Compulsive Scale (Y–BOCS), which was mentioned earlier, is a comprehensive interview schedule that covers the main types of obsessions and compulsions. This allows the therapist to estimate the severity of the disorder, particularly the extent to which it interferes with the person's life. A brief self-report version of this has also been developed, and is often used in clinical assessment.

Other scales

A scale for assessing compulsive ordering and related behaviour has been developed recently. It is called the Symmetry, Ordering, and Arranging Questionnaire (SOAQ), and is reproduced in Appendix 5.

Instruments for assessing related problems

The therapist may also use other inventories to measure depression, anxiety, phobias, and so on, if there is an indication that these are relevant in a patient's clinical presentation. As noted previously, depression tends to be closely linked to obsessions and compulsions, and many therapists include it in routine assessment. The most widely used screening instrument for assessing depression is the Beck Depression Inventory (BDI). Developed by Aaron T. Beck and his colleagues, it comprises twenty-one items covering areas such as mood, self-esteem, sleep, appetite, feelings of guilt, sex drive, suicidal ideas, and so on. For each item, the patient is asked to indicate whether he has experienced the affect or change in behaviour and, if so, to what degree. Scores of 0–3 are obtained for each item, yielding a possible maximum of 63. Scores above 10 are taken as showing the presence of mild depression, scores above 16 indicating moderate depression, and scores above 25 indicating severe depression. These cut-off points are not absolute and are only used as a rough guide.

For assessing general anxiety, there are several instruments, including the Beck Anxiety Inventory which, like the BDI, has twenty-one items each scored from 0 to 3. The total score is again 63.

Psychophysiological assessment

Psychological measures are sometimes undertaken with obsessive–compulsive patients. The activity of the autonomic nervous system, especially heart rate and skin conductance, may be measured under various conditions—e.g. while exposed to triggers, and after carrying out a compulsive ritual. While such measures are valuable for research, their usefulness in routine clinical assessment is limited. In most clinical settings patients will not be asked to undergo these recordings.

Assessment for evaluating therapy

In a systematic therapeutic approach, the patient will be assessed in some or all of the above ways at several points in time: before treatment begins, after a period of therapy, at the end of therapy, and at follow-up, usually six and twelve months later. In this way the patient's progress can be ascertained formally and methodically. The numerical scores, in particular, help to highlight the changes in the patient. For example, assuming successful therapy, a patient whose MOCI score was 21 at initial assessment may have a score of 7 at the six-month follow-up. A situation that evoked a discomfort level of 90 (on a 0–100 scale) before therapy may not provoke more than 10 after therapy. The frequency of hand-washing, which was twelve times a day on average before therapy, may now be only twice per day.

Of the instruments available, the Y–BOCS is considered particularly useful for assessing the progress of therapy.

9
Obsessive–compulsive disorder in children

Obsessive–compulsive disorder can occur in childhood. It is estimated that between 0.5 and 2 per cent of children and adolescents can be affected by the disorder. In most respects the symptoms and features resemble those seen in adults. It usually takes the form of repetitive, compulsive behaviour, and, as with adults, compulsive cleaning and compulsive checking are the most common manifestations. The compulsion to arrange objects and order tasks inflexibly and the drive for symmetry, are more frequently seen in children than in adults. The compulsion to count, and the compulsion to ask others to repeat utterances and actions, are also common in obsessive–compulsive children. Very often the compulsive behaviour—the checking, cleaning, and ordering—is carried out in an attempt to prevent or ward off harm. The child has an inflated fear of harm coming to parents, relatives, friends, or self, and tries to protect people by carrying out the compulsive activities. However, in some the compulsive behaviour has no such basis; instead, the compulsion is driven by a sense that 'it is not right' or 'it does not feel right'.

An 8-year-old girl spent long hours each day arranging and ordering all of her possessions, books and clothes in a fixed pattern as a means of preventing her mother from dying. The family had been involved in a motor vehicle accident that severely injured the patient's mother, leaving her bleeding and semi-conscious. Prior to the accident the child had been 'nervous' and this quality was greatly increased after the accident. She was easily startled, clinging, and tearful, and her sleep was disturbed. After the accident she changed from a neat and tidy child into a compulsive checker with a drive to keep her possessions in a strict, inflexible order. When this overwhelming need to protect her mother and other relatives became evident, she was reassured in a few sessions, accompanied by her parents, that the family was in no particular danger and that her father and mother were reliable, strong, and responsible. As the child's feelings that she bore special responsibility for protecting the family subsided, the compulsions faded out.

Differences from superstitions

Some of the beliefs and associated repetitive actions may resemble super-stitions that drive the child to look for safety for himself and family or for lucky charms and sayings that will bring good luck. Unlike superstitious behaviour, however, childhood obsessive–compulsive disorder is concerned exclusively with negative thoughts, with threats of harm which then lead to the wish to carry out protective actions. Unlike superstitious ideas obsessive–compulsive disorder always involves emotion, especially sadness and fear, and it is not regarded by the child as being the same as a superstition. Obsessive–compulsive disorder is not easily open to rational analysis and to rational change.

In some instances it is difficult to distinguish between obsessive–compulsive ideas and behaviour and superstitious beliefs and behaviour. However, as Table 6 illustrates, there are some simple tests that can be applied in trying to make the distinction between superstitious beliefs and habits and obsessive–compulsive problems.

Table 6 Comparison of obsessive–compulsive problems and superstitions in children

Obsessive–compulsive problems	Superstitious beliefs and behaviour
Compulsions are driven, repetitive behaviour which at times the child will attempt to resist and which are recognized by him as being excessive or irrational. Typical examples include repetitive, compulsive washing to remove dirt or germs. Incompletion of the compulsions, especially their interruption, can cause distress. The compulsions and their driving force are personal to the affected child and not shared by other children or members of the family	Concerned with good and bad luck, they are seldom resisted by the child, and rarely cause distress. Superstitions are irrational or magical beliefs that are shared by other children or adults. Unlike obsessions, they are not unique and personal

Features of childhood obsessive–compulsive disorder

The unwanted, intrusive, repugnant and recurrent thoughts (obsessions) that affect many of adult patients are seldom described by children. Two of the three major themes of adult obsessions, those that involve blasphemy and/or unacceptable sexual ideas, are rarely encountered. Fears of losing control and unwillingly harming people occasionally emerge in adolescence. Cognitive biases are seldom evident in children with bsessive–compulsive disorder.

As with adults, there is an association between obsessive–compulsive disorder and depression in children; the depression is as likely to follow the obsessive–compulsive disorder as to precede it. In cases of childhood obsessive–compulsive disorder a slight elevation of psychological problems is found in members of the family. Between 10 and 20 per cent of parents are likely to have experienced some form of anxiety disorder or mood disorder. The gender distribution is different from that in adult patients. There is a male to female ratio of 3 : 2. The age of onset appears to be earlier for boys than for girls. Roughly half of children with obsessive–compulsive disorder also have significant social fears, and a significant minority have eating problems. Up to a third of them are excessively perfectionistic.

In the prolonged study of the development of all 1,037 children born in Dunedin, New Zealand in 1972, 182 had at least one symptom of obsessive–compulsive disorder by the age of 11. Reassuringly, only eighteen still had any obsessive–compulsive disorder symptoms by the age of 21; that is, 90 per cent of the participants had lost their symptoms. As few of the children had received formal treatment, the findings suggest, reassuringly, that most young children do 'grow out of it'. However, the prospects can be troubling for those children who do not improve spontaneously during childhood. Without treatment, obsessive–compulsive disorder can become a chronic problem and, in severe cases, is incapacitating. One-third of adult cases report that their obsessive–compulsive disorder began in some form or other during child-hood. In the Dunedin study, those who developed severe obsessive–compulsive disorder showed a history of behavioural problems of various kinds during childhood. As with adult obsessive–compulsive disorder, the effect on the child's life can be serious. It can lead to social isolation, disruption of education, family conflicts, and a distressing brew of fear, sadness, and frustration.

Signs of the disorder

What are the signs of obsessive–compulsive disorder in children? The most obvious signs of an obsessive–compulsive problem in a child are behavioural.

If the child is seen to engage in intense repetitive checking, cleaning, or ordering for lengthy periods of time, and to do so in a way that interferes with or prevents ordinary activities such as studying, dressing, eating, bathing, etc. one needs to take notice. If this intense and repetitive behaviour is rigid and resistant to change, it may signal an obsessive–compulsive disorder, particularly if the child reacts emotionally to interruptions or interference with the activities (such as interfering with the fixed inflexible patterning and arranging of their possessions). More often than not the child will be unable to explain the reason for the behaviour and may resort to saying, 'I must do it *right*', or 'I have to keep doing it until it feels *right*'. Accompanying signs may be depression and/or social withdrawal or isolation. As the compulsions can demand a great deal of time, the child may leave other tasks undone, often be late, and seemingly very slow to complete activities. In cases in which perfectionism is prominent, the child devotes meticulous attention to tasks, especially studying, and may have to produce numerous copies of assignments before he is satisfied. These children show an inflexibility and often are late, with a strong tendency to procrastinate. They resist suggestions that their perfectionistic behaviour is excessive and self-defeating, and stubbornly oppose the adoption of more flexible aims and habits.

Some case examples

A 14-year-old boy complained of a variety of troubling obsessions, indecisiveness, repeated checking, and washing his hands up to thirty times per day. Many of his obsessions concerned harm coming to others (e.g. being involved in a car accident) and violent images of a catastrophic nature. In response to the obsessions, he felt compelled to wash his hands repeatedly. In addition, he felt driven to repeat whatever action he had been engaged in when the obsession occurred (e.g. repeatedly packing his school bag, repeatedly putting on his shoes). At school he had to re-read book chapters four times, and repeatedly check and correct all of his written work (he had used so much correcting fluid that his teacher was obliged to ban it completely). The tedium and stress involved in trying to get his homework 'just right' was so great that he began avoiding it totally. He ate his food in a ritual manner, and strictly avoided sharing food with anyone else because of his fears of harm.

A 12-year-old-girl was frightened of a range of objects which she felt might be dangerously contaminated, and took care to avoid any household items which contained warnings on the label, sticky substances, urine on lavatory seats, and so on. She was also fearful of raw meat and a variety of possible sources of germs. The underlying fear was that harm might come to her, other people, or pets. She also complained of obsessional impulses that she might cause harm, express obscenities, or steal. She attempted to control the distress caused by these fears and obsessions by widespread avoidance and by compulsive cleaning and checking activities. Her checking was taking up to three hours per day, and the cleaning two hours per day. In addition, she repeatedly sought reassurance from her parents that they were safe.

From the age of 8, Norman displayed a powerful and widespread fear of germs and diseases. Whenever he felt contaminated he engaged in repetitive, intensive washing of hands, which showed clear signs of abrasions resulting from the excessive washing. He also spent a good deal of time checking the safety of household electrical appliances. As the fear of contamination spread, he became increasingly avoidant and finally was unable to attend school.

Glynis was an intensely preoccupied and serious child from an early age. At the age of 7 it became apparent to her parents that she was widely fearful and constantly dreaded that 'something horrible will happen to me'. In order to protect herself from the anticipated but vague catastrophe, she became exceedingly cautious and inflexible. She had to prepare and wear her limited range of clothes in a carefully prescribed order and fashion, rarely strayed from her 'safe' routes, ate in a slow and inflexible manner, spent two hours per day showering, and so on.

Nine-year-old Michael developed a serious fear of germs, washed a lot, and ate a very narrow range of foods that had to be 'hygienically' prepared (he inspected all of the cutlery meticulously). He insisted on precision in all matters, large and small, and was easily provoked to anger if his family failed to comply with his needs and fears.

Diagnosis and assessment

It is important to bear in mind that the child rarely complains of compulsions or obsessions. Even when parents, friends, and teachers see signs of significant obsessive–compulsive disorder-like problems, the affected child is likely to underplay or even deny the problem. Naturally this can obscure the identification of childhood obsessive–compulsive disorder. In order to tackle this problem of differing reports, Dr Roz Shafran and her colleagues developed a self-report scale, the Children's Obsessive–Compulsive Inventory (Ch-OCI), to be filled in by the child, and a version for the parent to fill in on the child's behalf.

The Ch-OCI consists of two parts. The first deals with compulsive behaviour (called 'habits' in the instrument). There are ten items. Examples are:

- I spend a lot of time every day checking things over and over again.
- I always count, even when doing ordinary things.

The second part is about obsessions (called 'thoughts' in the instrument). Again there are ten items. Examples are:

- I often have bad thoughts that make me feel like a terrible person.
- I can't stop upsetting myself about death, going round in my head, over and over again.

For each part, an additional section enquires about the extent of the most upsetting habits, and the most prominent thoughts.

The parents' version of the Ch-OCI is exactly the same except that the parent is asked to fill it in, to reflect the habits/thoughts of their son or daughter.

The Ch-OCI is reproduced in Appendix 6.

Unlike the standard clinical diagnostic interviews for childhood obsessive–compulsive disorder, which typically yield a gap between the reports given by the child and the parent, the Ch-OCI tends to produce comparable results for the child and parent. However, the scale is merely a supplement to the standard diagnostic interview techniques and the children's version of the Yale scale for measuring obsessive–compulsive disorder (see page 100). The children's version of the Yale interview schedule (CY–BOCS) is the most widely used instrument specifically constructed to assess obsessive–compulsive disorder and is an extension to the standard adult version (Y–BOCS). The use of the CY–BOCS is generally preceded by the standard-ized interview schedule, the child and the parent version of the Diagnostic Interview Schedule (DISC), which tests for a range of psychological and psychiatric problems, including depression.

If a child displays intense inflexible compulsive behaviour of the type set out above, and if there are accompanying signs, then the possibility of obsessive–compulsive disorder is worth considering. In addition to seeking a medical/psychological opinion, completion of the Ch-OCI may be useful.

In addition to the standardized interviews and formal tests that comprise the assessment of obsessive–compulsive disorder in children, it is usually necessary to have a period of observation of the child's behaviour, especially if it is thought that the child is underplaying the difficulties. As already mentioned, in many instances the obsessive–compulsive disorder is accompanied by other problems such as social anxiety and depressed mood. Some children with obsessive–compulsive disorder are extremely demanding and controlling, and tend to become upset and angry when their compulsions are interrupted or blocked by others. At times they may become aggressive and, in extreme examples, control the entire family in an attempt to deal with their anxiety and the associated compulsive behaviour.

Some diagnostic problems

Tourette syndrome

Diagnostic problems sometimes arise from a confusion between the purposeful, intentional compulsive behaviour such as cleaning and checking, and repetitive but purposeless twitches or tics. In some cases of severe tic disorders, such as the Tourette syndrome (see pp. 30–31), compulsive behaviour is evident. Among the majority of children with obsessive–compulsive disorder, the occurrence of major and disruptive tics is not common. However some children with obsessive–compulsive disorder do have the Tourette syndrome. Interestingly, differences have been reported between obsessive–compulsive children who also have the Tourette syndrome and those who do not. Those with the Tourette syndrome have more touching, counting, and blinking compulsions, and fewer cleaning compulsions, than those who do not have the Tourette syndrome.

Autism

Obsessive–compulsive problems in children also need to be distinguished from childhood autism, also called 'autistic disorder'. Some of the clinical features of autism superficially resemble symptoms of obsessive–compulsive disorder. These include: a strict adherence to rigid routines or rituals, repetitive motor behaviour (such as specific movements of hands or whole-body movements), and preoccupation with details of things which to others appear irrelevant or unimportant. Autistic children dislike change, and tend to maintain, and protest against attempts by others to alter, sameness.

While these factors seem to overlap with some of the symptoms of childhood obsessive–compulsive disorder, autistic children also have other, prominent deficits. These include impairment of social interactions, including, in many cases, an inability to respond to others' emotions, and difficulties or abnormalities in communication. These deficits are not part of obsessive–compulsive problems in children.

Autism is essentially what child psychologists and psychiatrists call a developmental disorder—i.e. it is a disorder that first appears in infancy or childhood. In the case of autism, diagnostic criteria stipulate that delays or abnormal functioning in social interaction, language, or symbolic/ imaginative play are detected before the age of 3.

Treatment

The literature on the treatment of children with obsessive–compulsive disorder is limited, largely because of the relatively small number of cases reported. The best treatment seems to be the same kind of psychological therapy used with adult patients—especially a combination of exposure and response prevention for those with overt rituals. The specifically cognitive elements used commonly in the treatment of adults have limited relevance in the treatment of children, in particular the younger ones. Medication may play a useful role, especially if the child is depressed. Parents are involved in the treatment and given advice and help on how to deal with the child's problem behaviour, especially his demands for things to be done in a certain way, or repeated requests for reassurance. The parents should act in a comforting but firm manner. Some parents may also need help with basic child management techniques. Work with the family is an important part of therapy, since family members need a good deal of help and support. Formal family therapy may be undertaken in addition to the specific behavioural treatment; indeed, some therapists consider this to be an integral part of therapy. The child's school and the teachers are also commonly involved in the treatment programme, because it is important to ensure consistency in the way adults respond to the child's behaviour. In some cases, the severity of the problem makes a period in hospital necessary.

Much work is currently being done in childhood obsessive–compulsive problems, and there is every reason to expect significant advances in treatment in the future.

10
Some practical advice

Is there a problem?

Although the majority of people have obsessional experiences and compulsions, for most people these are not major problems. The person is not particularly worried or concerned about them, and neither seeks nor wants assistance. There is no evidence that Samuel Johnson (see p. 12) was particularly bothered by his ritual concerning the number of steps to take when approaching a door. If you check your gas cooker twice before you leave home every morning, or tend to be a bit concerned about cleanliness and make sure that you wash your hands before each meal, there is no need to feel that there is something faulty or abnormal in your behaviour. Similarly, if you get the occasional unwanted thought like 'God does not exist', or an occasional mental image of a corpse in a coffin, again that need not worry you. It is not the mere presence of obsessions and/or compulsions that warrants concern; rather, it is whether they interfere with your life and activities in a significant way, and whether they cause you distress.

Some key questions

So, the questions that you need to ask yourself are ones such as the following:

- Are there things that you very much like or need to do, but are prevented from doing because of your obsessions and/or compulsions?
- Do you find yourself constantly avoiding certain things, places, people, or other activities as a result of obsessions and/or compulsions?
- Has your job or other occupation become difficult as a result of obsessions and/or compulsions?
- Do you get very upset by the content or frequency of the obsessions?

- Are you very unhappy about the nature of your compulsive rituals— e.g. are they bizarre or very excessive, or do they make you open to ridicule by others?
- Do you find yourself spending a great deal of time engaging in compulsive behaviour or obsessional ruminations?
- Is your compulsive behaviour a significant nuisance or hindrance to others?
- Are your difficulties creating problems in your personal relationships?

If your answer to any of these questions is 'yes' then it is possible that your obsessions and/or compulsions merit attention, and you may wish to consider doing something about them.

Concern about a family member

The same considerations apply when a spouse, partner, or any other relative or friend notices compulsive behaviour, excessive reassurance seeking, and so on in a person. It may be that someone takes a little more time in the bath than other members of the family, or has his room arranged in a particularly neat way. This should not worry the family. On the other hand, if the behaviour is very excessive, the person consistently makes unreasonable demands on the family, or it is clear that his work is seriously affected, then the family may be justifiably worried and want to initiate some action. Many people with obsessive–compulsive problems attempt to hide their difficulties from their families and friends, so it may not become clear to them in the early stages that a problem exists.

Seeking help

Once it is recognized that there is a problem, the best course of action is to seek professional advice. In some cases, it may be possible to deal with the difficulties without recourse to such help, but in most cases seeking professional advice is the best course of action.

Finding a therapist

The first step is to go to your own doctor and explain the problem. There is no need to fear that he will think you are peculiar or crazy; he will recognize that this a problem requiring help, and refer you to a professional who is skilled in dealing with it. This will usually be a clinical psychologist or a psychiatrist or, where available, a nurse therapist with special training in dealing with problems of this kind. Your doctor may himself give you advice and treatment, if he has a particular interest and experience in this area.

The therapist to whom you are referred is more likely than not to be someone with a cognitive behavioural approach, in view of the success of this approach in dealing with these problems. If the doctor is unaware of a suitable therapist locally, you or your doctor could contact the British Association for Behavioural and Cognitive Psychotherapies (BABCP), who will advice on therapists in the area. This will, however, be unnecessary in most cases, because the local psychiatric service will normally be able to channel you to a suitable practitioner. Most of these therapists are in the National Health Service in Britain but if, for some reason, you prefer to see someone privately, the BABCP will be able to advise. General advice on the services of clinical psychologists and psychiatrists may be obtained from their respective professional organizations, the British Psychological Society and the Royal Collage of Psychiatrists. Advice is also obtainable from MIND, which is the National Association for Mental Health, and several other organizations, including First Steps to Freedom, No Panic, and OCD Action.

In the United States, the Obsessive–Compulsive Foundation, set up a few years ago, provides information and advice for sufferers of obsessive–compulsive disorder and their families and friends. Many have found contact with the foundation, which is a voluntary and non-profit-making organization, to be extremely useful. Another organization that provides useful information and advice on this disorder is the Anxiety Disorders Association of America.

The addresses of these and other relevant agencies are given in Appendix 7.

The therapist's assessment

When you go for your initial assessment, the therapist will try to collect as much relevant information as possible. It may well take more than one interview for him to complete the assessment. The information he is likely to require will include the kind of detail we have discussed in the previous chapters, especially the one on assessment. Your therapist may also give you some questionnaires, checklists, or inventories to complete. He may ask you to carry out short tests. For example, if your problems include a fear of contamination by dirt, he may ask you to touch, with the open palm of your hand, table surfaces, tops of cupboards, door handles, and so on. Or, if you have horrible thoughts and impulses that you might stab someone, the therapist may ask you to hold a knife or a pair of scissors in your hands and to describe to him what thoughts, images, and impulses come to your mind at the time. He may also give you some homework in the form of keeping a diary or record of your problems as they occur in the next week or two. Cooperate with this even if you think it is a chore. The therapist may also want to see you at home, to see for himself what your problems are and how you cope. Naturally, this will depend on the nature of the problem and on how much time the therapist has at his disposal. Many therapists nowadays, if they can find the time, are likely to include a home visit as a part of the assessment, especially when you have rituals that you carry out at home or home-related avoidance behaviour.

Planning and implementation of therapy

In the planning the treatment programme, your therapist will discuss with you what areas to concentrate on, what targets to aim for, and how to set about achieving those targets. The involvement of a family member as a co-therapist is likely to be discussed, and he or she will be included in the discussion of homework arrangements and related matters. If the problem is difficult to manage on an out-patient basis, hospitalization for a limited period will be considered. Hospital treatment will include not only your therapist, but also nurses and other professionals. A family member may also be invited to take part in some hospital sessions; they can then help with the next stage of therapy away from the hospital. If your treatment is entirely on an out-patient basis, which is quite possible, the therapist may conduct, or arrange for, some additional sessions in your home. These domiciliary sessions can be extremely valuable, and many therapists consider them to be essential. Irrespective of this, you will be given plenty of advice and instructions about what you should and should not do at home. For example, you may be told that you should disarrange your desk and wardrobe and leave them like that. Implementation of such instructions will be left to you and/or the family member acting as co-therapist.

Do not be surprised if the therapist asks you to continue to keep regular records of what happens at home, since this information is valuable in monitoring your progress. He may wish to go over your home records and discuss them in detail at the beginning of each session.

If an exposure and response prevention programme is undertaken in an out-patient clinic, at least some of your sessions with the therapist are likely to be quite long. This is because the therapist will want to ensure a significantly long response prevention period to allow your discomfort to dissipate. Also, part of each session is likely to be devoted to discussions between you and the therapist. He will want to explore your fears of disaster, the significance you attach to the obsession, your difficulties at home or work, what you really think will happen if you do not ritualize, how responsible you feel for harm that may happen, and so on. There may also be imaginal exposure. For example, if your fears include a worry that, if you do not check the gas taps three times, the whole house will burn down, your therapist may ask you to close your eyes and imagine such a scene vividly. Such imaginal exposure may be conducted in several sessions. At times, real-life exposure to a particular situation may be preceded by you being asked to go through the experience in your imagination.

In summary, your sessions are likely to be lengthy (especially at the start), and also to include various activities. The main ingredient will be exposure and response prevention, if your problems are treatable in this way, along with detailed homework instructions. If your main problems are of a different kind, such as repetitive unwanted thoughts with no associated overt rituals, then your treatment sessions will take a different form. Even then, homework is very likely to be part of the programme. If your main problem is slowness, then much of the therapy may well be home-based.

A further word is needed about the involvement of family members. The role that a co-therapist plays will be clearly defined and detailed, and specific instructions given. This is in order to avoid any ambiguity leading to conflict. The family will also receive instructions about not complying with your demands, or requests for reassurance. All these will have been discussed fully and openly, with your active involvement. Any doubts or queries you may have, you should discuss fully with the therapist.

The need for cooperation

It is important that you cooperate fully with the therapist, your co-therapist, and any others involved. Carrying out some of the instructions may be very difficult for you (e.g. the task of rubbing your hands on the kitchen floor and then not washing your hands) but it is important that you do your best to comply. The difficulty will, normally, get progressively less with more and more sessions. If you find that you are sometimes tempted not to comply fully—for example, you may feel like washing your hands secretly, or touching the floor only very lightly with the tips of your fingers—it is important that you discuss it with the therapist. Remember that therapy for these problems is essentially a joint venture. Your therapist has no magic cure, and without your cooperation can achieve nothing. Half-hearted cooperation will only waste your time as well as your therapist's. So discuss any problem with him. He will appreciate your difficulties, and discuss them with you. If, for some reason, you wash when you are not supposed to, you can remedy this to some extent by immediately 'recont-aminating' yourself by touching the contaminating object.

It can, in short, be difficult work. But, if you are motivated to get over your problems, you will find that, with the help of your therapist, you can keep it up. Occasional lapses should not be seen as failure. Do not let them discourage you. Once you begin to see the results of your efforts, you will be very glad that you underwent the therapy. It will make a big difference.

Adjustment problems

When you gradually improve with treatment, you may well find that you need to adjust to a new lifestyle, especially if your problems have been long-standing. You will find that you have much free time, and probably not many activities to fill that time with. You will need to develop new ways of filling your time, and perhaps new activities. You may need to re-establish old contacts and relationships. Your therapist will usually discuss these matters with you and also give advice and counselling on how to make these adjustments. It is possible that your family members will also have similar problems, if their lives had been moulded around your problems for years.

After therapy

When you have achieved improvement, do not expect to be totally free of symptoms. What usually happens, in cases where the problem involves interrelated obsessions and compulsions, is that the compulsive behaviour is brought under control with the exposure and response-prevention treatment fairy rapidly, but the obsessional ideas may not go away at the same time. They may linger on, but without arousing much discomfort or leading to a strong compulsive urge. After a time, you will notice them less and less, and they may well disappear altogether. You may still have minor residual problems, and perhaps continue to be a more anxious person than many others. Do not be too disappointed at this—you can learn to cope with these. With major disabling problems largely out of the way, such coping will be easier.

Once successfully treated, the chances of a major relapse are not very high. However, there may be minor lapses. At times of stress (e.g. with problems at work, a death or a serious illness in the family, and so on) the chances of symptoms reappearing may be somewhat increased. You can minimize the effects of stress if you use strategies to cope with situations. Relaxation practice is one such strategy (see Appendix 1). If the symptoms of the disorder do reappear, you will notice these signs early on, and can give yourself a few booster sessions using the principles of treatment you are now familiar with. It is not unusual for a therapist to have arranged boosters at various time intervals. He will, in any case, have arranged for follow-up appointments for you, in order to ascertain how well you are doing and to give you help and support as needed. If you feel that you are losing control again, contact your therapist, even if there is no follow-up arrangement. It must be reiterated, however, that after a carefully planned therapy programme has been successfully carried out, the chances of the problems re-emerging in full-blown form are limited.

The use of drugs

It is possible that your therapist will consider drugs as part of the treatment. As only a medical practitioner can prescribe drugs, if your therapist is not a doctor he will ask your own doctor, or a psychiatrist he works with, to consider this. The most likely circumstances for this would be if your mood is depressed and this has either stalled your progress or is making it difficult for you even to engage in therapy. In such cases, antidepressant medication may be prescribed (see pp. 89–91). Or, your doctor may want to start the treatment of your obsessions and compulsions with a drug. Whatever drug is prescribed, it is very important that you tell the doctor what other medicines you are taking, any allergies that you have, whether you are pregnant, and so on. Make sure you get very clear instructions about the dosage and what foods and drinks (if any) to avoid, and discuss possible side-effects. Commonly prescribed antidepressant drugs, including clomipramine, have several well-known side-effects (see pp. 90–91). These are, however, reversible: when the drug is stopped, they will clear up.

Two other points are worth bearing in mind with regard to medication. The first is that antidepressant drugs do not produce results immediately—it may be weeks before any improvement is seen. Secondly, if you are treated just with an antidepressant drug and no cognitive behavioural treatment, improvements in your obsessive–compulsive symptoms may diminish or disappear when you come off the drug.

If you are on anxiety-reducing drugs at the time of seeking help from a cognitive behaviour therapist, he may suggest that you discuss with the prescriber whether the drugs should be withdrawn or at least reduced, before therapy begins. The prescribing doctor will be fully involved in these discussions and decisions. If you are in the habit of drinking large amounts of alcohol, you will be asked to reduce this.

Brain surgery

It is extremely unlikely that your therapist will recommend brain surgery—unless your problems are very chronic, totally resistant to other forms of therapy, and you are incapacitated by them, this will not even be considered. If psychosurgery is proposed, you do not have to agree to accept this procedure and you would be well advised to seek a second or even a third opinion, if you wish to consider it. Even then, the final decision will be yours alone. Normally, this form of treatment is best avoided. When it is suggested, the very fullest consultation and discussion are needed.

Self-treatment

Is it possible for someone with obsessive–compulsive disorder to treat himself? Research done in a major London hospital has shown that some patients who treat themselves do almost as well as those treated by therapists; but, in this case, the assessment and initial advice came from qualified and experienced therapists. Can you do the whole thing yourself, from start to finish? If the problem is not very severe, and if there are no other complications, this is not impossible. You need a commitment to the planned treatment, and a systematic approach. However, if you are seriously depressed, then you should not attempt this. Also, if you habitually take a lot of alcohol and drugs such as benzodiazepines, self-help should not be attempted without first consulting your doctor. The nature of the problem is also important. Clear overt rituals and clear avoidance behaviour that are well defined are likely to be more amenable to self-treatment than incessant ruminations or complicated mental rituals. You need to check whether yours is the right kind of problem to treat yourself.

Selecting targets

The first requirement is to select and specify a small number of targets related to your problem. Consider what aspects of the problem you need to improve upon most, then formulate the target very specifically. For example, you may decide that one of your targets will be 'to be able to empty the kitchen waste bin into the main dustbin each night' or 'to be able to leave home every morning without checking the gas and electricity more than once'. These are good, workable targets. More global targets such as 'to get rid of my fear of contamination' or 'to be free of repeated checking and doubting' are less useful, and hard to make use of in treatment programmes. So, be specific in setting targets for yourself.

You should not attempt to tackle too many targets at the same time. It is advisable to begin with just one, or two at the most. As therapy progresses, you can add on new targets to your programme as you master the original ones.

Getting the help of others

If at all possible, enlist the help of a co-therapist, to whom you will explain your problems and the therapy plan fully. The co-therapist may be your wife or husband, a relative living at home or nearby, or a friend or trusted colleague, for certain kinds of targets. It is a good idea to write down with your co-therapist exactly what his role will be, and your commitments to him (e.g. not to argue when he reminds you to do something). Obviously, if your problems involve others being asked to comply with your demands or to provide you with reassurance and so on, then they need to be told not to comply any more, in relation to the targets you are working on.

Record-keeping

Keeping records is important. They make it easier for you to see your progress, and to identify any difficulties that may arise. For a start, it will be useful just to monitor yourself for a two-week period, using a form like the one in Figs 2 and 3 (see pp. 97 and 98). This will give you a record of the extent of the problem prior to treatment. For recording your actual treatment, use another record sheet—like the specimen form given in Fig. 4. Figure 5 is an illustration of a completed sheet. You will see how all the main details can be recorded on such a form systematically and without too much effort.

In addition, for each exposure session, you can monitor and record your discomfort and urge to ritualize in graphic form. An easy-to-use format for this is provided in Fig. 6. An example of a completed form is given in Fig. 7.

Implementing therapy

For your exposure sessions, you will need to allow some time, even up to three hours for major tasks. It is best not to finish a session while your discomfort is still high, so make sure that you have enough time. For many other tasks, much less time may be needed. It is best to start with difficult but manageable tasks. If you start with tasks that are too difficult, you may end up getting discouraged. For some targets, especially where the problem consists of time-consuming rituals, a gradual, step-by-step approach may be appropriate. If, for example, one of your problems is spending over an hour in folding and hanging your clothes at night, your target may be 'folding hanging my clothes at night in ten minutes'. If you are happy to attempt this from the very fist day, then fine. On the other hand, if it is too much to attempt at first, you could break this target down into a series of tasks; you will set yourself the task of completing the activity in

Date: Target:[1]

Task[2]	
Time	
Any help[3]	
Discomfort felt[4]	
Urge to ritualize[5]	
Outcome[6]	

1   The particular compulsion treated.
2   Specific task undertaken.
3   Was a co-therapist involved? Who?
4,5 Rated on a 0–100 scale.
6   Details of what happened.

Figure 4 A specimen record sheet for a treatment session, blank

progressively shorter times each night. For example, on day one, forty
minutes; on day two, thirty minutes; day three, twenty minutes, and so on.
Remember, however, that a long series of very small steps is not a very efficient way of going about your targets, so do try to start at a fairly high level.

Always remember the basic principles of exposure and response prevention—the less you avoid things because of your obsession or through
fear of having to ritualize, the better. So in addition to your formal
programme, make sure that you confront your difficulties or obstacles
rather than avoid or escape from them. Non-avoidance is a sound general
principle to bear in mind.

Date: 10 October   Target:[1] Hand–washing

Task[2]	Take kitchen waste bin downstairs and empty into main bin. Clean and reline kitchen bin and place it back in kitchen. Rub hands on clothes and arms. No washing or wiping
Time	9.15 a.m.
Any help[3]	Frances (girlfriend) accompanied me downstairs and back, and encouraged me to rub my hands on my clothes and arms.
Discomfort felt[4]	80 (half-hourly ratings on separate form)
Urge to ritualize[5]	75 (as above)
Outcome[6]	Kept my hands loosely clenched and sat in a corner for some time. Gradually felt better. Had some tea about 10.30. Read the newspaper. On the whole, it went well.

1   The particular compulsion treated.

2   Specific task undertaken.

3   Was a co-therapist involved? Who?

4,5   Rated on a 0–100 scale.

6   Details of what happened.

Figure 5 An example of a record sheet for a treatment session, completed

If you tend to be generally anxious, and experience marked physical signs of anxiety, then a useful addition to your self-treatment programme would be some training in relaxation. If you do this, make sure you find the time to practice regularly. How to go about teaching yourself to relax is discussed in Appendix 1.

Appraisal of problem

How you see your problem is important. Having obsessions and compulsions is not particularly unusual or rare, so remind yourself that lots of people have them and that having them does not mean that you are crazy

Discomfort and urge to ritualize (0–100)

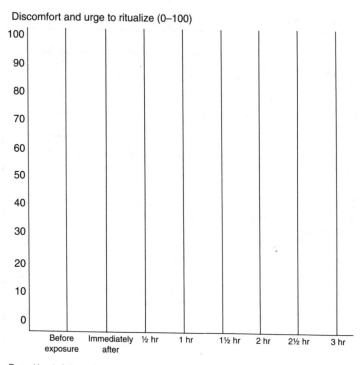

Record level of discomfort with an X, and strength of urge to ritualize with an O; connect each set of entries.

Figure 6 A specimen sheet for recording discomfort and urge to ritualize in an exposure and response-prevention session

or mad, or that you are going mad. The main problem is the interference they cause in your life, and this is what your treatment programme is intended to reduce.

A word of caution

A word of caution is needed about self-treatment: even if much of the therapy is done by yourself, it is useful to have your problems assessed by, and receive advice from, a qualified therapist. He will advise you on whether or not a self-therapy programme is suitable, and may agree to see you from time to time to review your progress. So, do not undertake it entirely on your own unless your problems are relatively minor ones, or you have no suitable therapist available. As noted earlier, once you have been seen by

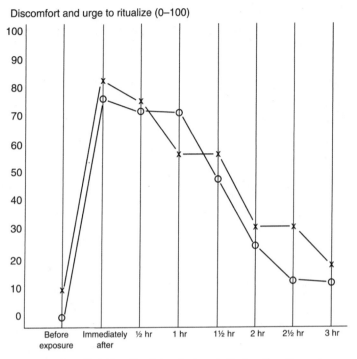

Record level of discomfort with an X, and strength of urge to ritualize with an O; connect each set of entries.

Figure 7 An example of a completed sheet for recording discomfort and urge to ritualize in an exposure and response-prevention session

a therapist and a treatment plan is drawn up, a good deal of the actual work will be done by you anyway. In that sense, much therapy for these problems nowadays necessarily involves self-treatment. The principles outlined in this section will, we hope, be of some use to you, even if you are treated by a professional therapist.

A word of hope

Remember that obsessive–compulsive disorder is a treatable condition. Much progress has been made in the past four decades in helping people to get over these problems. Very many people with this disorder have benefited from treatment and now lead normal lives. With the right advice, appropriate treatment, and your own effort, obsessive–compulsive disorder can be overcome.

appendix 1

Learning to relax: a simple guide

Do your relaxation exercises in a quiet room, at a time when you are not likely to be disturbed. Sit comfortably in a armchair. Make sure that your clothes are not tight. Remove belts, spectacles, and shoes.

Learn to relax by first tensing and then relaxing various muscle groups of the body, one at a time. Keep your eyes closed throughout. At each step, keep the muscles tensed, quite hard, for 6–8 seconds. Concentrate on the muscles, and notice the tension. Then relax the muscles, and keep them relaxed for 45–50 seconds. Again, concentrate on the muscles, and notice how the feelings of relaxation differ from those of tension. You can learn to time yourself quite easily by slowly counting for the first few times. Remember to repeat the tense–relax cycles for each muscle group before you move on to the next. When you tense a group of muscles, take a breath and hold it until you relax the muscles, releasing the breath slowly as you relax.

Given below is the order in which to tense and relax the various muscle groups. For each muscle group, a strategy for making them tense is given. For some, alternative strategies are suggested. Before you actually start the proper relaxation exercises, learn the way in which each muscle group can be effectively tensed. Try out one at a time, and master it. Where alternatives are suggested, decide which one is going to be your regular strategy. Once this is done, you can begin the actual sessions.

1. *Right hand and forearm.* Tense the muscles by making a tight fist; or, try pressing the inner part of the finger tips against the base of the thumb. Relax by slowly opening the hand.

2. *Right biceps.* Tense the muscles by pushing your elbow into the arm of the chair, or by pressing elbow and the upper arm into the side of the rib cage. Relax by returning to original position.

3. *Left hand and forearm.* As for the right hand and forearm.

4. *Left biceps.* As for right biceps.

Note: If you are left handed, do steps 3 and 4 first, followed by steps 1 and 2.

5. *Forehead.* Tense by raising your eyebrows as high as possible with your eyes still closed. Relax by returning your eyebrows to normal position.

6. *Upper cheeks and nose.* Tense by squinting and screwing up your eyes, and wrinkling the nose. Relax by returning to normal position.

7. *Lower cheeks and jaws.* Tense by clenching your teeth together and pulling back the corners of your mouth. Relax by unclenching the teeth and bringing mouth back to normal.

8. *Neck.* Tense by pulling your chin into your chest, but not quite touching it. Relax by returning to original position.

9. *Shoulders and chest.* Tense by raising and pulling your shoulder blades towards each other. Relax by returning to original position.

10. *Stomach and abdomen.* Tense by pulling in your stomach and abdomen as much as you can. You can also tense these muscles by pushing out your stomach and abdomen. Relax by returning to original state.

11. *Right leg.* Tense by straightening the whole leg from the hip, parallel to the floor. Relax by lowering and resting the leg on the floor again.

12. *Right foot.* Tense by pushing your heel into the floor and curling your toes upwards—i.e. towards you. Relax by returning to original position.

13. *Left leg.* As for right leg.

14. *Left foot.* As for right foot.

Note: If your dominant leg is the left one, do steps 13 and 14 before 11 and 12.

15. *Whole body.* Tense as many of the above muscle groups as you can all at once, making yourself into a 'ball of tension'. You will find that you can tense most of the muscle groups together; in fact, if you use the tension strategies suggested above, there will be only two of these items that you will not be able to do while doing everything else. One is the raising of the eyebrows, but the eyebrows can be tensed by wrinkling them when you screw up the eyes. Second is the pushing of your heels into the floor, but with your legs stretched, you will still be able to curl your toes up towards you.

Remember that each step is to be done twice, including the last 'all body' step. Remember also to take in a breath and hold it when the muscles are kept tense and to release the breath as you relax the muscles.

After the whole sequence is completed, continue to sit in a relaxed state for several minutes. At this point, you may imagine a pleasant scene, like a peaceful beach or a flower garden. With practice, when you become more skilled in relaxing yourself, you will find that the actual exercises become quite easy. After some weeks of practice, you will be able to relax yourself by simply tensing and relaxing the entire body—that is, the last step of the sequence given above—without going through the various individual steps. With even more practice, many people acquire the ability to relax very effectively simply by concentrating on making their muscles relaxed without having first to tense them.

If you prefer to do your relaxation exercises lying down on a bed or on the floor, you need only minor changes to the above programme. For each leg, what you will need to do is to raise it from the bed or floor to form an angle of about 30 degrees. Relax by lowering the leg and resting it on the bed or floor.

There is no particular time of the day when relaxation should be practised, but avoid doing it when you are very sleepy, so that you do not sleep while relaxing. Try to do it daily in the early stages, so that you will become good at it.

Different authors suggest different sequences of muscle groups for relaxation exercises. There is no particular advantage of one over the others. What is important is to use a sequence that is fairly logical, as the one given here, not a random or haphazard one. You should use the same sequence regularly, so it will be easier to learn and master it.

There are cassette tapes available commercially that give recorded instructions for relaxation training. Using one of these can be useful in the early stages, but it is important to wean yourself gradually away from the cassette since the aim is to learn to relax without any external aid.

The following are some good cassettes that are commercially available.

Relax and enjoy it, by Robert Sharpe, which is available from Aleph One Ltd, The Old Courthouse, High Street, Bottisham, Cambridge CB5 9BA, UK.

Self-help relaxation, by Jane Madders, available from Relaxation for Living Ltd, 29 Burwood Park Road, Walton-on-Thames, Surrey KT12 5LH, UK.

How to relax, by Rachel Norris and Christine Cuchemann, which comes with *Managing anxiety: a user's manual*, by Helen Kennerley, available from the Psychology Department, Warneford Hospital, Oxford OX3 7JX, UK.

The relaxation tapes (and videos), produced by First Steps to Freedom, 7 Avon Court, School Lane, Kenilworth, Warwickshire CV8 2GX, UK.

appendix 2

Antidepressant drugs

Drug	UK brand name	US brand name
Tricyclics		
Amitriptyline	Triptafen, Lentizol	Elavil
Clomipramine	Anafranil	Anafranil
Imipramine	Tofranil	Tofranil, Janimine
Nortriptyline	Allegron	Aventyl, Pamelor
Monoamine oxidase inhibitors		
Phenelzine	Nardil	Nardil
Tranylcypromine	Parnate	Parnate
Selective serotonin re-uptake inhibitors		
Citalopram	Cipramil	Celexa
Fluoxetine	Prozac	Prozac
Fluvoxamine	Faverin	Luvox
Paroxetine	Seroxat	Paxil
Sertraline	Lustral	Zoloft

Note: This is not complete list.

appendix 3

The Maudsley Obsessional–Compulsive Inventory (MOCI)

(See Appendix 4 for scoring instructions.)

Instructions

Please answer each question by putting a circle around the TRUE or the FALSE following the questions. Work quickly and do not think too long about the exact meaning of the question.

1.	Avoid using public telephones because of possible contamination.	TRUE	FALSE
2.	I frequently get nasty thoughts and have difficulty in getting rid of them.	TRUE	FALSE
3.	I am more concerned than most people about honesty.	TRUE	FALSE
4.	I am often late because I can't seem to get through everything on time.	TRUE	FALSE
5.	I don't worry unduly about contamination if I touch an animal.	TRUE	FALSE
6.	I frequently have to check things (e.g. gas or water taps, doors, and so on) several times.	TRUE	FALSE
7.	I have a very strict conscience.	TRUE	FALSE
8.	I find that almost every day I am upset by unpleasant thoughts that come into my mind against my will.	TRUE	FALSE
9.	I do not worry unduly if I accidentally bump into somebody.	TRUE	FALSE
10.	I usually have serious doubts about the simple everyday things I do.	TRUE	FALSE
11.	Neither of my parents was very strict during my childhood.	TRUE	FALSE

Continued

Continued

12.	I tend to get behind in my work because I repeat things over and over again.	TRUE	FALSE
13.	I use only an average amount of soap.	TRUE	FALSE
14.	Some numbers are extremely unlucky.	TRUE	FALSE
15.	I do not check letters over and over again before mailing them.	TRUE	FALSE
16.	I do not take a long time to dress in the morning.	TRUE	FALSE
17.	I am not excessively concerned about cleanliness.	TRUE	FALSE
18.	One of my major problems is that I pay too much attention to detail.	TRUE	FALSE
19.	I can use well-kept toilets without any hesitation.	TRUE	FALSE
20.	My major problem is repeated checking.	TRUE	FALSE
21.	I am not unduly concerned about germs and diseases.	TRUE	FALSE
22.	I do not tend to check things more than once.	TRUE	FALSE
23.	I do not stick to a very routine when doing ordinary things.	TRUE	FALSE
24.	My hands do not feel dirty after touching money.	TRUE	FALSE
25.	I do not usually count when doing a routine task.	TRUE	FALSE
26.	I take rather a long time to complete my washing in the morning.	TRUE	FALSE
27.	I do not use a great deal of antiseptics.	TRUE	FALSE
28.	I spend a lot of time every day checking things over and over again.	TRUE	FALSE
29.	Hanging and folding my clothes at night does not take up a lot of time.	TRUE	FALSE
30.	Even when I do something very carefully, I often feel that is not quite right.	TRUE	FALSE

References

Hodgson, R. and Rachman, S. (1977). Obsessional-compulsive complaints. *Behaviour Research and Therapy,* **15**, 389–95.

appendix 4

Scoring key for the Maudsley Obsessional–Compulsive Inventory

Instructions

Score 1 when a response matches that of this key and 0 when it does not; maximum scores for the five scales are, therefore, 30, 9, 11, 7, 7.

Question	Total obsessional score	Checking	Washing	Slowness–repetition	Doubting–conscientiousness
Q1	TRUE	.	TRUE	.	.
Q2	TRUE	TRUE	.	FALSE	.
Q3	TRUE	.	.	.	TRUE
Q4	TRUE	.	TRUE	TRUE	.
Q5	FALSE	.	FALSE	.	.
Q6	TRUE	TRUE	.	.	.
Q7	TRUE	.	.	.	TRUE
Q8	TRUE	TRUE	.	FALSE	.
Q9	FALSE	.	FALSE	.	.

Continued

Continued

Question	Total obsessional score	Checking	Washing	Slowness–repetition	Doubting–conscientiousness
Q10	TRUE	·	·	·	TRUE
Q11	FALSE	·	·	·	FALSE
Q12	TRUE	·	FALSE	·	TRUE
Q13	FALSE	·	·	·	·
Q14	TRUE	TRUE	·	·	·
Q15	FALSE	FALSE	·	·	·
Q16	FALSE	·	FALSE	FALSE	·
Q17	TRUE	·	·	·	TRUE
Q18	FALSE	·	FALSE	·	·
Q19	FALSE	·	FALSE	·	·
Q20	TRUE	TRUE	·	·	·
Q21	FALSE	·	FALSE	·	·
Q22	FALSE	FALSE	·	FALSE	·
Q23	FALSE	·	FALSE	·	·
Q24	FALSE	·	·	FALSE	·
Q25	FALSE	·	·	·	·
Q26	TRUE	TRUE	TRUE	·	·
Q27	FALSE	·	FALSE	·	·
Q28	TRUE	TRUE	·	FALSE	·
Q29	FALSE	·	·	·	·
Q30	TRUE	·	·	·	TRUE

appendix 5

The Symmetry, Ordering, and Arranging Questionnaire*

*This instrument has been produced with the kind permission of Dr. A. S. Radomsky.

Please circle a number from 0 to 4 to indicate how much you agree with each statement:

		Not at all	Slightly	Moderately	Very	Extremely
1.	I feel upset if my furniture or other possessions are not always in exactly the same position.	0	1	2	3	4
2.	Other people think I spend too much time ordering and arranging my belongings.	0	1	2	3	4
3.	It is essential that I arrange my clothing in a particular and specific way.	0	1	2	3	4
4.	I am more at ease when my belongings are 'just right'.	0	1	2	3	4
5.	I must keep my papers, receipts, documents, etc. organized according to a specific set of rules.	0	1	2	3	4
6.	It is important that my belongings are placed in a symmetrical and evenly distributed way.	0	1	2	3	4
7.	If someone accidentally disturbs my belongings, however slightly, I become bothered or upset.	0	1	2	3	4

Continued

Continued

	Not at all	Slightly	Moderately	Very	Extremely
8. I feel compelled to arrange my possessions until it feels 'just right'.	0	1	2	3	4
9. When I think that my belongings are out of place, I am uncomfortable or anxious.	0	1	2	3	4
10. When I put my things away, I feel compelled to do it carefully and precisely.	0	1	2	3	4
11. The furniture in my home must be in exactly the 'right' spot.	0	1	2	3	4
12. I feel calm and relaxed only when objects around me are organized and placed correctly.	0	1	2	3	4
13. I feel compelled to arrange cans or boxes of food on my kitchen shelves in a specific way.	0	1	2	3	4
14. When I see that my belongings are out of place, I become anxious until I can arrange them properly.	0	1	2	3	4
15. I feel compelled to arrange objects so that they are balanced and evenly spaced.	0	1	2	3	4
16. I feel calm/at ease only when my surroundings are neat and tidy.	0	1	2	3	4
17. Even when my home is messy, I keep things organized according to a specific set of rules.	0	1	2	3	4
18. Things in my home have a proper and exact place.	0	1	2	3	4
19. I cannot concentrate unless things are in the right place.	0	1	2	3	4
20. I don't like to disturb objects once they are properly arranged.	0	1	2	3	4

The score is the sum of item scores. Scores above 30 are in the high range; low scores fall in the range of 0–10.

References

Radomsky, A. S. and Rachman, S. (2004). Symmetry, ordering and arranging compulsive behaviour. *Behaviour Research and Theryapy*, **42**, 893–913.

appendix 6

Children's Obsessive–Compulsive Inventory

(This instrument has been reproduced here with the kind permission of Dr R. Shafran.)

TO BE COMPLETED BY THE YOUNG PERSON

Date:_____   Age:_____   Sex: Male/Female

Ch-OCI: Part 1

Each of the following questions asks you about things or 'habits' you feel you have to do although you may know that they do not make sense. Sometimes, you may try to stop from doing them but this might not be possible. You might feel worried or angry or frustrated until you have finished what you have to do. An example of a habit like this may be the need to wash your hands over and over again even though they are not really dirty, or the need to count up to a special number (e.g. 6 or 10) while you do certain things.

Please answer each question by putting a circle around the number that best describes how much you agree with the statement, or how much you think it is true of you. Please answer each item, without spending too much time on any one item. There are no right or wrong answers.

Example: I feel that I must check and check again that the stove is turned off, even if I don't want to do so.	Not at all 1	Somewhat 2	A lot 3

How much do you agree with each of the following statements?	Not at all	Somewhat	A lot
1. I spend far too much time washing my hands over and over again.	1	2	3
2. I feel I must do ordinary/everyday things exactly the same way, every time I do them.	1	2	3
3. I spend a lot of time every day checking things over and over and over again.	1	2	3
4. I often have trouble finishing things because I need to make absolutely sure that everything is exactly right.	1	2	3
5. I spend far too much time arranging my things in order.	1	2	3
6. I need someone to tell me things are alright over and over again.	1	2	3
7. If I touch something with one hand, I feel I absolutely <u>must</u> touch the same thing with the other hand, in order to make things even and equal.	1	2	3
8. I always count, even when doing ordinary things.	1	2	3
9. If I have a 'bad thought', I always have to make sure that I immediately have a 'good thought' to cancel it out.	1	2	3
10. I am often very late because I keep on repeating the same action, over and over again.	1	2	3

Please try to think about the three <u>most</u> upsetting **habits** that you feel you **have** to do and **can't stop**. For example, feeling that you have to wash your hands far too often, or repeating the same action over and over, or constantly checking that the doors and windows are shut properly.

1)_____

2)_____

3)_____

How much time do you spend doing these habits? Please circle the answer that best describes you.

0	1	2	3	4
None	Less than 1 hour a day (occasionally)	1–3 hours a day (part of a morning or afternoon)	3–8 hours a day (about half the time you're awake)	More than 8 hours a day (almost all the time you're awake)

How much do these habits get in the way of school or doing things with friends? Please circle the answer that best describes you.

0	1	2	3	4
Not at all	A little	Somewhat	A lot	Almost always

How would you feel if prevented from carrying out your habits? How upset would you become? Please circle the answer that best describes you.

0	1	2	3	4
Not at all	A little	Somewhat	A lot	Totally

How much do you try to fight the upsetting habits? Please circle the answer that best describes you.

0	1	2	3	4
I always try to resist	I try to resist most of the time	I make some effort to resist	Even though I want to, I don't try to resist	I don't resist at all

How strong is the feeling that you have to carry out the habits? Please circle the answer that best describes you.

0	1	2	3	4
Not strong	Mild pressure to carry out habits	Strong pressure to carry out habits; hard to control	Very strong pressure to carry out habits; very hard to control	Extreme pressure to carry out habits; impossible to control

How much have you been avoiding doing anything, going any place, or being with anyone because of your upsetting habits? Please circle the answer that best describes you.

0	1	2	3	4
Not at all	A little	Somewhat	A lot	Almost always

Ch-OCI: Part 2

In this section, each of the questions asks you about *thoughts, ideas, or pictures* that keep coming into your mind even though you do not want them to do so. They may be unpleasant, silly, or embarrassing. For example, some young people have the repeated thought that germs or dirt are harming them or other people, or that something unpleasant may happen to them or someone special to them. **These are thoughts that keep coming back, over and over again, even though you do not want them.**

Please answer each question by putting a circle around the number that best describes how much you agree with the statement, or how much you think it is true of you. Please answer each item, without spending too much time on any one item. There are no right or wrong answers.

Example: I often have the same upsetting thought about death over and over again.	Not at all	Somewhat	A lot
	1	2	3

How much do you agree with each of the following statements?	Not at all	Somewhat	A lot
1. I can't stop thinking upsetting thoughts about an accident.	1	2	3
2. I often have bad thoughts that make me feel like a terrible person.	1	2	3
3. Upsetting thoughts about my family being hurt go round and round in my head and stop me from concentrating.	1	2	3
4. I always have big doubts about whether I've made the right decision, even about stupid little things.	1	2	3
5. I can't stop upsetting thoughts about death from going round in my head, over and over again.	1	2	3
6. I often have mean thoughts about other people that I feel are terrible, over and over again.	1	2	3
7. I often have horrible thoughts about going crazy.	1	2	3

Continued

Continued

How much do you agree with each of the following statements?	Not at all	Somewhat	A lot
8. I keep on having frightening thoughts that something terrible is going to happen and it will be my fault.	1	2	3
9. I'm very frightened that I will think something (or do something) that will upset God.	1	2	3
10. I'm always worried that my mean thoughts about other people are as wicked as actually doing mean things to them.	1	2	3

Please list the three most severe **thoughts** that you often have **and can't stop thinking about.** For example, thinking about hurting someone, or thinking bad things about God.

1)_____

2)_____

3)_____

How much time do you spend thinking about these things? Please circle the answer that best describes you.

0	1	2	3	4
None	Less than 1 hour a day (occasionally)	1–3 hours a day (part of a morning or afternoon)	3–8 hours a day (about half the time you're awake)	More than 8 hours a day (almost all the time you're awake)

How much do these thoughts get in the way of school or doing things with friends? Please circle the answer that best describes you.

0	1	2	3	4
Not at all	A little	Somewhat	A lot	Extreme

How much do these thoughts bother or upset you? Please circle the answer that best describes you.

0	1	2	3	4
Not at all	A little	Somewhat	A lot	Extreme

How hard do you try to stop the thoughts or ignore them? Please circle the answer that best describes you.

0	1	2	3	4
I always try to resist	I try to resist most of the time	I make some effort to resist	Even though I want to, I don't try to resist	I don't resist at all

When you try to fight the thoughts, can you beat them? How much control do you have over the thoughts? Please circle the answer that best describes you.

0	1	2	3	4
Complete control	Much control	Moderate control	Little control	No control

How much have you been avoiding doing anything, going any place, or being with anyone because of your thoughts? Please circle the answer that best describes you.

0	1	2	3	4
Not at all	A little	Somewhat	A lot	Almost always

Scoring of the Ch-OCI

Part 1: Compulsions ('Habits')

- Add together the scores of the ten items (score 1, 2, 3) to get the compulsions symptom total.
- Add together the scores of the first five impairment items (score 0, 1, 2, 3, 4) to get the total score for impairment caused by compulsions. The final item (avoidance) is not included.

Part 2: Obsessions ('Thoughts')

- Add together the scores of the ten items (score 1, 2, 3) to get the obsessions symptom total.
- Add together the scores of the first five impairment items (score 0, 1, 2, 3, 4) to get the total score for impairment caused by obsessions. The final item (avoidance) is not included.

The range of possible scores are:

compulsions:	symptom score	10–30
	impairment score	0–20
obsessions:	symptom score	10–30
	impairment score	0–20

Note: The parents' version is the same as the child's version, except for obvious wording changes.

Reference

Suafran, R., Frampton, I., Heyman, I., Reynolds, M., Teachman, B., and Rachman, S. (2003). The preliminary development of a new self-report measure for OCD in young people. *Journal of Adolescence*, **26**, 137–42.

appendix 7

Addresses of useful organizations

UK

British Association for Behavioural and Cognitive Psychotherapies
Globe Centre
PO Box 9
Accrington BB5 2DG
www.babcp.org.uk

British Psychological Society
St Andrews House
48 Princes Road East
Leicester LE1 7DR
www.bps.org.uk

Royal College of Psychiatrists
17 Belgrave Square
London SW1X 8PG
www.rcpsych.ac.uk

MIND, National Association for Mental Health
22 Harley Street
London W1N 2ED
www.mind.org.uk

OCD Action
Aberdeen Centre
22–24 Highbury Grove
London N5 2EA
www.ocdaction.org.uk

No Panic
93 Brands Farm Way
Randlay
Telford TF3 2JQ
www.no-panic.co.uk

First Steps to Freedom
7 Avon Court
School Lane
Kenilworth
Warwickshire CV8 2GX
www.first-steps.org

Triumph Over Phobia (TOP U.K.)
PO Box 1831
Bath BA2 4YW
www.triumphoverphobia.com

USA

Association for Advancement of Behavior Therapy
305 Seventh Avenue, 16th Floor
New York, NY 10001–6008
www.aabt.org

American Psychiatric Association
1000 Wilson Boulevard
Suite1825
Arlington, VA 22209–3901
www.psych.org

American Psychological Association
750 First Street, NE
Washington DC 20002–4242
www.apa.org

Obsessive–Compulsive Foundation, Inc.
676 State Street
New Haven, CT 06511
www.ocfoundation.org

The Anxiety Disorders Association of America
8730 Georgia Avenue
Suite 600
Silver Spring, MD 20910
www.adaa.org

National Institute of Mental Health (NIMH)
Office of Communications
6001 Executive Boulevard
Room 8184 MSC 9663
Bethesda, MD 20892–9663
www.nimh.nih.gov

Canada
Canadian Psychiatric Association
260–441 MacLaren Street
Ottawa
Ontario K2P 2H3
cpa@cpa-apc.org
www.cpa_apc.org

Canadian Psychological Association
151 Slater Street
Suite 205
Ottawa
Ontario K1P 5H3
www.cpa.ca

Canadian Mental Health Association
8 King Street East
Suite 810
Toronto
Ontario M5C 1B5
www.cmha.ca

Anxiety Disorders Association, British Columbia (ADABC)
4438 West 10th Avenue
Suite 119
Vancouver
British Columbia V6R 4R8
www.anxietybc.com

Australia
Australian Psychological Society
PO Box 38
Flinders Lane Post Office
Melbourne
VIC 8009
www.psychsociety.com.au

Royal Australian and New Zealand College of Psychiatrists
309 La Trobe Street
Melbourne
VIC 3000
www.ranzcp.org

Australian Association for Cognitive and Behaviour Therapy
www.aabct.org

Mental Health Association NSW Inc.
ada@mentalhealth.asn.au

CRUFAD (Clinical Research Unit for Anxiety and Depression)
St Vincent's Hospital
299 Forbes Street
Darlington
Sydney NSW 2010
www.crufad.org
www.crufad.com

appendix 8

Some useful reading

Technical

There are several technical books providing good accounts of obsessive–compulsive disorder. Here are some:

Barlow, D. H. (2002). *Anxiety and its disorders* (revised 2nd edn). Guilford Press, New York.

> This is a comprehensive book on the whole range of anxiety disorders, and has a particularly useful chapter on obsessive–compulsive disorder. Recently revised and expanded.

Clark, D. A. (2004). *Cognitive-behavioral therapy for OCD*. Guilford Press, New York.

> Comprehensive, excellent account.

Clark, D. M. and Fairburn, C. G. (eds) (1997). *The science and practice of cognitive behaviour therapy*. Oxford University Press, Oxford.

> An excellent volume that covers developments in psychological treatment, including the treatment of obsessive–compulsive disorder.

Craske, M. (1999). *Anxiety disorders*. Westview Press, Boulder, CO.

> Another comprehensive discussion of the whole range of anxiety disorders.

McLean, P. D. and Woody, S. R. (2001). *Anxiety disorders in adults*. Oxford University Press, New York.

> A lucid account of the nature and treatment of obsessive–compulsive disorder and other anxiety disorders.

Menzies, R. G. and de Silva, P. (eds) (2003). *Obsessive–compulsive disorder: theory, research and treatment*. Wiley, Chichester.

> This edited volume gives up-to-date information on all aspects of obsessive–compulsive disorder and its treatment.

Rachman, S. (2002). *The treatment of obsessions*. Oxford University Press, Oxford.

> This book gives an original approach to the understanding and treatment of obsessions.

Rachman, S. and Hodgson, R. (1980). *Obsessions and compulsions.* Prentice-Hall, Englewood Cliffs, NJ.

> This book provides a discussion of the field of obsessive–compulsive disorder. It describes the nature of obsessions and compulsions, gives an account of the authors' research, and comments on theoretical issues.

Swinson, R. P., Antony, M. M., Rachman, S., and Richter, M. A. (eds) (1998). *Obsessive–compulsive disorder: theory, research, and treatment.* Guilford Press, New York.

> An edited volume with authoritative chapters on many aspects of the disorder.

For a briefer account see:

de Silva, P. (1994). Obsessions and compulsions: investigations and treatment. In *The handbook of clinical adult psychology* (2nd edn), (ed. S. J. E. Lindsay and G. E. Powell), pp. 51–91. Routledge, London.

An excellent account of cognitive behavioural treatment is found in:

Salkovskis, P. and Kirk, J. (1997). Obsessive–compulsive disorder. In *Science and practice of cognitive behaviour therapy,* (ed. D. M. Clark and C. G. Fairburn), pp. 179–208. Oxford University Press, Oxford.

For a more detailed discussion of therapy, see:

Kozak, M. J. and Foa, E. B. (1996). Obsessive–compulsive disorder. In *Sourcebook of psychological treatment manuals for adult disorders,* (ed. V. B. Van Hasselt and M. Hersen), pp. 65–122. Plenum Press, New York.

For a detailed discussion of theoretical approaches see:

Jakes, I. (1996). *Theoretical approaches to obsessive–compulsive disorder.* Cambridge University Press, Cambridge.

Non-technical

Useful and readable accounts, including self-help advice, are found in numerous books, including the following:

Foa, E. B. and Wilson, R. (1991). *S.T.O.P. obsessing! How to overcome your obsessions and compulsions.* Bantam Books, New York.

Steketee, G. and White, K. (1990). *When once is not enough: help for obsessive compulsives.* New Harbinger, Oakland, CA.

For an excellent personal account of obsessive–compulsive phenomena, and an overview of the whole field from a general reader's perspective, see:

Toates, F. and Coschug-Toates, O. (2002). *Obsessive–compulsive disorder: practical, tried-and-tested strategies to overcome OCD* (2nd edn). Class Publishing, London.

For an account of another anxiety disorder and its treatment, see:

Rachman, S. and de Silva, P. (2004). *Panic disorder: the facts* (2nd edn). Oxford University Press, Oxford.

index